Concise Dictionary of

CONTEMPORARY HISTORY

Concise Dictionary

of

CONTEMPORARY HISTORY

Compiled by
SHERWIN BURICKSON

With a Foreword by
HARRY ELMER BARNES

PHILOSOPHICAL LIBRARY
New York

D
419
.B8
1959

9098203
B958c

FOREWORD
by
Harry Elmer Barnes

The proto-human and human past is continually being
pushed further back. Only recently, we have heard that
what appears to be the skeleton of a direct ancestor of
man was discovered in an Italian coal mine. This speci-
men is estimated to have lived some ten million years ago.
The origins of what can accurately be called civilized life
in the ancient Near East are now dated somewhere between 7,500 and 10,000 B.C., as against the 3,000-5,000
B.C. which was the accepted figure at the turn of the century. The materials to be studied in tracing the course of
civilization are constantly being expanded.

All of this could enable mankind to learn more lessons
from history so as better to understand the present and
more intelligently to plan the future. Whether the human
race is able to learn anything from history is a moot question. Hegel is said to have observed that the main lesson
to be learned from history is that mankind is incapable of
learning anything from history. The major events of the
twentieth century might appear to many to provide im-
pressive confirmation of Hegel's dolorous generalization.
In our age of ever more complex technology and social
organization, and of potential nuclear, chemical, and bac-
terial warfare, it is becoming increasingly evident that if
humanity cannot learn the main lessons provided by
history it is doomed to either rapid extermination or
gradual disintegration and elimination.

The most important lessons that could be learned from
history are those supplied by contemporary history, notably the record of the preceding hundred years which mark
the origins of the fourth great world revolution through
which humanity is now passing. The effort to draw precise
and useful analogies with periods in the distant past is
always absorbing but they are usually less dependable
than they are interesting and stimulating. Opponents of
the New Deal were wont to draw analogies between it
and the reforms of the Emperor Diocletian. A broad
analogy was evident and sound, namely, that both the

Roman Empire in the days of Diocletian and the United States (in common with the Western world as a whole) in the 1930's were passing through a period of major institutional decay and readjustment. But to try to draw a precise analogy between the reforms of Diocletian and Roosevelt was obviously highly misleading.

Diocletian lived in a pre-industrial society, a scarcity handicraft economy, and an imperial political order that was beginning to pass into a condition of proto-feudalism —the *colonate*. Roosevelt was seeking to deal with a machine age industrialism, with a technology which was already threatening us with over abundance unless better methods of distributing its products were provided, and with the defects of a representative and democratic political system quite unknown to Diocletian. To take one concrete example: historians are now agreed that the most important cause of the decline of the Roman Empire was the lack of transportation facilities equal to the needs of a vast and far-flung empire which were far beyond what could be supplied by foot soldiers, horses, chariots or the primitive sea-faring navigation of those days, fairly represented by the mishaps of St. Paul on his way to Rome. Today, we are challenged by transportation facilities which are perhaps too profuse, complex, efficient, and speedy to be successfully handled by man. The Romans had trouble reaching Britain or Persia; we are now seeking to reach the moon and the nearer planets.

If, however, analogies with a distant past can only be valid in a very generalized and sweeping sense, the facts of the last hundred years are indispensable to anyone who seeks intelligently to approach any of the major problems of our time. The culture of 1958 probably differs more from that of 1858 in many vital aspects than that of 1858 differed from the age of Alexander the Great. Those who might regard this as a slight exaggeration surely could not successfully challenge the statement that the changes in many of the more fundamental phases of human life and society since 1758 are more striking than those between 1758 and those of Hammurabi or Rameses II. This is the basic reason for the transcendent importance of contemporary history in any effort to understand our age and to solve its problems effectively. The exploits of ancient military geniuses, medieval romances and chivalry, and the adventures of early modern buccaneers may provide vivid prose and exciting reading but they tell us little about how to get the most out of our machinery and to distribute its products effectively, how to make democracy work and avoid totalitarian "waves of the future," or how to prevent nuclear wars of extermination.

One of the more useful applications of history to human intelligence is to portray our epoch of human experience against the broad panorama of the entire civilized human past. If we do this, it is evident that we are passing through the fourth great world revolution in the drama of history. The first was that provided by what we call the Dawn of History, the passage from primitive tribal society and a stone culture to a metal culture, civil society, and a written language. The second came when ancient imperial society in the West broke up and was replaced by an agrarian, feudal, Catholic civilization between the reigns of Diocletian and Charlemagne. The third arrived when medieval civilization broke down after 1450 and was followed by the rise of the national state, the expansion of Europe and the Commercial Revolution, the rise of capitalism, the beginnings of mechanical industry, the schism within Christianity, and the growth of the liberal tradition in education, politics and law. The fourth world revolution, through which we are now passing, started to get under way about the time of the first World War, when the cultural pattern of the nineteenth century began to be subjected to strains and stresses roughly comparable o those met by feudalism, manorialism, the guilds, and Catholicism in the three centuries following 1450.

This sweeping and critical revolution of our day was brought into being by what cultural historians and sociologists call "cultural lag," namely the disparity between our up-to-the-minute technology and our archaic body of institutions that date in their origins somewhere between primitive society and the close of the eighteenth century. All of our main public problems, and many difficulties of private life, arise directly or indirectly out of this cultural lag. The basic task of our time is to solve its challenge and close the great gap or gulf between technology and institutions. If we solve this problem, mankind can speedily pass into an era of world peace and at least a material utopia, with its challenge to move ahead to those cultural levels which Plato emphasized as being beyond the reach of pigs, who deserve plenty of food and decent shelter. If we fail to respond successfully to this challenge brought to us by cultural lag, we face either long and dreary years of cold war tensions that will deprive us of many of the fruits of technological efficiency, or a hot war of nuclear extermination which may destroy the human race or, at the least, set civilization back for a thousand years. The longer the nuclear war is postponed, the greater the probability that it will utterly exterminate humanity if it does come.

It is for this dramatic and critical reason that contemporary history is not only the most important era in the historical experience of mankind but the one which veritably holds the key to the very destiny of the human race. To have a competent grasp of the scope, nature and complexities of contemporary society would require the perusal of many volumes. Many cannot take the time for this, and even those who have already done so have constant need for a handy book of reference to which they can turn at once to recall or identify facts and figures of significance in the recent past. This constitutes the real value of this DICTIONARY OF CONTEMPORARY HISTORY which will certainly receive and deserve the gratitude of those alert and fortunate enough to make use of it.

A

A.B.C. Powers Argentina, Brazil, and Chile, three major South American nations which have acted as mediators in disputes involving Latin America. They mediated the dispute between the United States and Mexico at Niagara Falls, Canada in 1914, the first conference of its kind in the Americas. In 1915, by the ABC Treaty, a permanent mediation Commission was established which, in that year, settled a dispute between Colombia and Peru. In 1935 these powers mediated the Gran Chaco Dispute between Bolivia and Paraguay.

Abu Dhabi One of the independent trucial states located on the Arabian peninsula. British influence extends over it because of its important oil deposits.

Acheson, Dean Gooderham (1893-) Statesman. b. Connecticut. Graduated Yale University (1915) and Harvard Law School (1918); practiced law; appointed Undersecretary of the Treasury (1933); Under Secretary of State (1945-47); after World War II was a strong supporter of the UNITED NATIONS; international relief programs, and the TRUMAN DOCTRINE; appointed Secretary of State by TRUMAN (1949-1953); he was a constant target of attack by Senate investigating committees, and for his policy toward the Soviet Union.

Addis Ababa Capitol of Ethiopia. Captured by Italian armies in May, 1936. Ethiopian Emperor, HAILE SELASSIE made an appeal to the League of Nations but in vain. On April 6, 1941, the capitol was taken from the Italians by the Allies and Selassie was restored to his throne from which Mussolini had driven him five years earlier.

Aden A colony of Great Britain located on the Arabian peninsula. It has strategic importance as a refinery center for Near Eastern oil.

1

Adenauer, Dr. Konrad (1876-)   The leader and founder of the Christian Democratic party in the German Federal Republic. In 1917 he was elected as Lord Mayor of Cologne. In 1933 HERMANN GÖRING removed him from all government posts because of his anti-Nazi sympathies. The Nazis arrested him a number of times prior to the end of the war. After World War II he was elected President of the Bonn Parliamentary Council (1948). In 1949 a Christian Democratic majority in West Germany appointed him Chancellor. In 1955 on a trip to Moscow he effected the release of Russian-held German prisoners-of-war. He is a strong supporter of a united Europe.

Afro-Asian Conference (1955)   A conference of Asian and African countries that was held in Bandung, Indonesia. Predominantly neutralist in the COLD WAR, the only important resolutions passed were those condemning colonialism in North Africa and in the Netherlands, New Guinea.

Alamein, el   City in northern Egypt, 70 miles from Alexandria to which the British army was driven back after the defeat at Cyrenaica. The Germans were so confident of victory that Mussolini was rushed from Italy to lead the conquering divisions into Cairo. Marshal Rommel delayed any fresh assault on the British Eighth Army at El Alamein until September, 1942, by which time the British position was greatly reinforced. Rommel's Afrika Korps was hurled back in the battle which followed marking the end of the German offensive in North Africa. The battle is regarded as the turning point of the war.

Albert I (1875-1934)   King of the Belgians (1909-34). He became a heroic world figure when the Germans invaded his country in 1914. He led his people in futile but heroic resistance. He spent the entire war at the head of his army. He did much to improve the social conditions in Belgium and the Belgian

2

Congo. He was killed in a rock-climbing accident in the Ardennes Mountains. He was succeeded by his son Leopold III.

Alexander I. (1888-1934) King of Yugoslavia (1921-1934). Commander-in-chief of the Serbian armies (1914-19). Prince regent of Serbia (1914-21) for his father, Peter I. He became king of the new kingdom of Yugoslavia in 1921. Because of disturbed conditions (1929) following the assassination of Stefan Radic he dismissed parliament and abolished the constitution. He did much to secure friendly relations with neighboring countries. He was assassinated in Marseilles, along with Foreign Minister Jean Louis Barthou of France, by a Croatian terrorist. He was succeeded by his son, Peter II (1923-). During Peter's minority, the country was ruled by a regency, headed by Prince Paul (1934-1941), Peter's uncle. Peter deposed the regent (March 1941), but left Yugoslavia (April 1941) after the German invasion. He has since been in exile, being prevented from resuming his throne by the TITO government.

Alexander, Harold Rupert Leofric George, Viscount Alexander of Tunis. (1891-) British field marshal. He has had a long military career, highlighted by service during the FIRST WORLD WAR and in the Northwest Province of India (1935). In the SECOND WORLD WAR he commanded the retreats at Dunkirk (1940) and in Burma (1942) before, as commander of the Middle East, he directed the conquest of North Africa. He then commanded the conquest of Sicily and the bitter fighting in Italy. Made field marshal (1944) and Supreme Allied Commander of the Mediterranean. In 1945 he was made Governor-General of Canada and (1946) he was created viscount.

Alfonso XIII (1886-1941) King of Spain (1886-1931). During his minority, Spain was under the regency of his mother (1886-1902). This period saw the loss

3

of the Philippine Islands and the last possessions in the New World. His reign was marked by rioting in Madrid and Barcelona over trouble in Morocco, by Spanish neutrality in WORLD WAR I, and by defeat in Morocco by Abd-el-Krim. He appointed PRIMO DE RIVERA premier (1923-29). This period was marked by riots, strikes, etc. He was finally forced to abdicate (1931) because of the Spanish Republic.

Algerian Independence Movement The great economic distinction between the French and the Arabs in Algeria has led to a large, active revolutionary underground intent upon the independence of Algeria. The most militant group is the NATIONAL LIBERATION FRONT. In 1956 the Algerians demanded a new constitution which would eventually bring them greater self-rule and eventual independence. When the French government turned down their demands, the Algerians rebelled.

Allied Control Committee (June 5, 1945) This Committee, which included GENERAL EISENHOWER, FIELD MARSHAL MONTGOMERY, and MARSHAL ZHUKOV, assumed full control throughout German territory following the surrender of Germany at the end of World War II. German territory, as it was on Dec. 31, 1937, was divided into Soviet, French, British, and American zones of occupation.

Allied Council for Japan The governing body administering the interests of the Allied Powers in Japan after WORLD WAR II. By the terms of the surrender of August 14, 1945 Japan agreed to her occupation until an ultimate peace treaty would be negotiated. General Douglas MacArthur was appointed Supreme Commander of the Allied Council which consisted of representatives of the United States, the Soviet Union, China, Australia, and the Philippine Islands. In 1951 General MacArthur was succeeded by General Matthew B. Ridgway. See Japan, Occupation of.

4

Allied High Commission The three man body consisting of high commissioners designated by the governments of the United States, Great Britain, and France, which exercises supreme authority in the GERMAN FEDERAL REPUBLIC. The powers of the commission are defined in the Occupation Statute. It is authorized to veto laws of the Republic and to exercise plenary powers over foreign policy, reparations, decartelization, security of allied occupation forces, disarmament, demilitarization, and control of the Ruhr. The Commission may also veto amendments of the Bonn Constitution. On April 28, 1949 it established the international Ruhr Authority to allocate the production of this industrial area. It has also approved federal statutes reorganizing the education system, agriculture, steel production, transportation and communication facilities and trade.

Allies, the The term applied to the Allied and Associated powers which defeated the CENTRAL POWERS in WORLD WAR I. The leading nations included the "BIG FIVE," the United States, Britain, France, Italy, and Japan. The other Allied powers were Belgium, Bolivia, Brazil, China, Costa Rica, Cuba, Haiti, Ecuador, Greece, Guatemala, Honduras, Liberia, Montenegro, Nicaragua, Panama, Peru, Portugal, Romania, Russia, San Marino, Serbia, Siam and Uruguay. The name is also occasionally applied to the members of the UNITED NATIONS in WORLD WAR II.

American Expeditionary Force The name given to the American armed forces overseas, in World War I.

American Note to Japan (November 26, 1941) This was the final answer given to Japan by Secretary of State Hull relating to the Far East. It proposed no foreign dominance in China and the discontinuance of Japanese expansion in southeast Asia and Oceania. The Japanese expecting these terms had already sent their task force on its way to Pearl Harbor.

5

Anarchism The political philosophy that equality and justice may be obtained only through the abolition of the state and its organs. In the twentieth century its adherents have been absorbed into the communist movement because of the Marxist construction that the state will eventually wither away.

Anglo-Egyptian Treaty (1936) A treaty of friendship at a time when England felt it necessary to consolidate her position against Germany. Previously Anglo-Egyptian relations had been strained. The treaty ended the British occupation of Egypt and made Egyptian independence definite.

Anglo-French Alliance (1938) A treaty creating unified commands for the armed forces of the two nations. It was to oppose the aggressive AXIS alliance that threatened imminent war.

Anschluss The German term applied to the forced union of Germany and Austria March 12-13, 1938. Schuschnigg, Chancellor of Austria, called for a referendum to reaffirm the independence of his country to be held March 13. On March 11, Germany submitted an ultimatum demanding the postponement of the plebiscite and the resignation of Schuschnigg. Unable to resist, Schuschnigg resigned in favor of Seyss-Inquart who immediately appealed to Germany for help to restore order. On March 13, Hitler proclaimed the union with Germany. On April 10, a plebiscite revealed a vote of 99.75% in favor of union with Germany.

Anti-Comintern Pact (Nov. 17, 1936) An agreement between Germany and the Japanese against communism and the Third Internationale. Italy and Spain signed this agreement at later dates, as did Hungary, Romania, Bulgaria, Slovakia, Croatia, Denmark, Finland, and the Japanese puppet governments of Manchukuo and Nanking.

Anti-Nazi Coalition (1934) The French Minister Barthou

6

created this coalition of Russia, France, Turkey, Czechoslovakia, England, and Italy, who was afraid (at the time) of German expansion southward.

Anti-Semitism (Hostility towards Jews) The most rampant form of minority discrimination in the twentieth century. Using the Jewish people as a collective scapegoat, the dictators of Eastern and Central Europe centered the economic frustrations of their subjects onto the Jews. The height of anti-Semitism occurred with the Nazi succession to power in Germany. Using fallacious racial theories, the Nazis declared the Jews a decadent racial group and placed the blame for all economic, social, and political ills on the Jewish population. Through a series of laws (see Nuremberg Laws) they systematically eliminated the Jews from virtually all professions and trades. All Jewish property was expropriated. Jews were forbidden from having any social intercourse with "Aryans." Hitler's final solution of the "Jewish Question" was the actual total extermination of the Jewish population in Germany and in subsequently conquered nations. This was done through an incredibly efficient system of concentration camps and gassing chambers. Between 1933 and 1945 the European Jewish population was almost totally destroyed. Half of world Jewry had been slaughtered by the followers of NATIONAL SOCIALISM in Germany. Anti-Semitism has been dormant in the post-World War II era, occurring sporadically in Eastern Europe and in Egypt after the ARAB-ISRAELI WAR.

Antonescu, Ion (1882-1946) Romanian general. As head of the fascist pro-German Iron Guard he forced Carol II to abdicate in 1940. Antonescu was the pro-German dictator of Romania (1940-44). He was executed in 1946.

Anzio Landings On January 22, 1944 the United States 6th Corps and the British 1st Division landed at Anzio below Cassino in Italy for the purpose of cutting German communications from Rome to Cassino and inducing General Kesselring to evacuate Cassino. The landings were unopposed. A general advance on January 30th met with only limited success. On February 8, 1945 the Germans counter-attacked and took Carroceto. They attacked again on February 16th and February 20th and inflicted heavy casualties upon the U.S. 3rd Division. Despite the great losses suffered by both armies, no material gains were achieved.

A.N.Z.U.S. (1951) A defense treaty signed by Australia, New Zealand, and The United States. It stated that an attack on any one party or its possessions in the Pacific would be an attack on all. It was prior to the more inclusive South East Asia Treaty Organization (s.e.a.t.o.) signed in 1954.

Apartheid A system of discrimination against non-whites practiced in The Union of South Africa.

Arab Federal State of Jordan and Iraq, the Created February 14, 1958. The Kings of both original states retain regional sovereignty. The head of the state is the king of Iraq. The legislature is composed of an equal number of representatives from the two original parliaments. Its creation closely followed that of the UNITED ARAB REPUBLIC. The recent revolt in Iraq dissolved this union.

Arab-Israeli War Upon the day of the creation of ISRAEL, May 14, 1948, the surrounding Arab nations, i.e. Egypt, Iraq, Jordan, Syria, and Lebanon, invaded the new state. Although hopelessly outnumbered, Israel routed all the Arab invaders, ending up with some slight increase in her own territory. Armistices were arranged in 1949. (See Tripartite Declaration.) War continued, however, in the form of Egyptian fedayeen infiltration forays. In the fall of 1956 the Israeli army counter-attacked against the fedayeen

8

positions on the GAZA STRIP. England and France intervened, supposedly, to save the Suez Canal from destruction. The United Nations finally negotiated an armistice and the Israeli army withdrew with a U.N. frontier force to guarantee the end of Egyptian infiltration attacks.

Arab League Created May 10, 1945. It is a diplomatic confederation of Egypt, Jordan, Lebanon, Saudi Arabia, Yemen, Libya, the Sudan, and Syria. Its basic idea is the creation of an "Arab Nation." It stands for anti-colonialism, COLD WAR neutralism, and the destruction of the State of Israel.

Arabic Crisis When two American lives were lost in the sinking of the British steamer **Arabic** (Aug. 19, 1915), the German Ambassador, von Bernstorff gave the so-called "Arabic pledge" that German submarines would not sink liners without warning and provisions for safety of noncombatants. During the remaining months of 1915 German U-boats concentrated on freighters.

Archangel-Murmansk Campaign An Allied invasion of Russia in 1917-1918 in which American troops participated. The campaign, under British command, was organized to assist the White Russians against the revolutionary Bolsheviks. By September, 1918 WILSON had ordered a total of 5100 U.S. troops to Arctic cities of Archangel and Murmansk to defend the harbor areas. By May, 1919 they had suffered 500 casualties. The last troops were withdrawn in July, 1919.

Ardennes Scene of German offensive beginning in March, 1918. In rugged fighting, beginning on the Somme, the Germans drove through this northern province of France on the Belgian border attemping to drive the Allies back to the Channel and split their armies in half. Aided by heavy fog they penetrated deep into Allied lines and were halted just short of the vital

9

communications center at Amiens. This situation closely resembled the German Army's last desperate offensive in the Ardennes in 1944.

Argonne Forest Scene of campaign in World War I in which the American troops marched north into the forest to form the right arm of a pincer. British troops formed the left attacking the Hindenburg line. After much hard fighting in this rugged terrain by more than a million American troops, the French city of Sedan was reached November 6, 1918 and while the German troops avoided the trap their lines crumbled.

Armed Ships Bill In an effort to prevent an overt act that would bring the U.S. into the war with Germany, Wilson asked Congress to authorize the arming of American merchant ships. The House passed the bill 403 to 13 but in the Senate isolationists filibustered the measure to the end of the session. The State Department found authority for the President to order the arming of merchant ships without congressional authorization. Ships sailing through war zones were armed after March 12, 1917 and were instructed by the Navy Department to take action against attacking submarines.

Armistice, the (Nov. 11, 1918) This agreement between the Allies and Germany ended the fighting in WORLD WAR I. It was signed at 11:00 A.M. in a railroad car in the forest of Compiègne. Within 14 days the Germans were to evacuate France, Belgium, Alsace-Lorraine, and Luxemburg; within a month, all territory west of the Rhine. Allied troops were to occupy the evacuated portion of Germany as well as the Rhine bridgeheads at Cologne, Coblenz, and Mainz to the depth of 30 kilometers east of the Rhine. The treaties of BREST-LITOVSK and Bucharest were to be renounced, and all German troops withdrawn from Russia, Romania, Turkey, and Austria-Hungary. A specified number of warships and all submarines were to be surrendered. Within two weeks the Allies were to receive 5,000 locomotives, 150,000 railway cars, and 5,000 motor trucks. All Allied prisoners of war were to be repatriated at once. The blockade of Germany was to remain in force. Large quantities of arms and artillery were to be surrendered.

Armistice between Austria-Hungary and the Allies Signed Nov. 3, 1918. By this agreement, Austria-Hungary withdrew from World War I. All Austro-Hungarian armies were to demobilized. Half of the equipment was to be surrendered. Disputed territory was to be evacuated. Allied forces were to occupy strategic points.

Arms Embargo A clause in the U.S. neutrality acts of 1935 and 1937 conferring upon the President the power to proclaim the existence of a state of war and invoke an embargo upon the export of arms, munitions, or implements of war to belligerent states or to neutral states for trans-shipment to belligerents. The President was empowered to enumerate such items. This provision was imposed in the Italo-Ethiopian war of 1934, 1935, the Spanish Civil War of 1936-1939, and in the Japanese-Chinese War from 1937 to the adoption of the "Cash and Carry" program in 1939.

Arsenal of Democracy The phrase used to describe the role of the United States as the munitions source of the UNITED NATIONS in WORLD WAR II.

Article X A section of the League of Nations Covenant where the members "undertake to respect and preserve as against external aggression the territorial integrity and existing political independence of all Members of the League."

Asquith, Herbert Henry (1852-1928) First Earl of Oxford and Asquith. English statesman. Liberal M.P. (1886-1918; 1920-24). Home secretary (1892-95). Chancellor of the exchequer (1905-08). Prime minis-

11

ter (1908-16). During his term as prime minister, the Liberal Party enjoyed some dramatic triumphs. The social-insurance program was instituted and the power of the House of Lords was broken. The First World War led to Asquith's downfall.

Aswan Dam An Egyptian project which caused cold-war tensions, due to President Nasser's playing off one side against the other for financial assistance to construct it.

Atlantic Charter, the (Aug. 14, 1941) A joint declaration by President Roosevelt and Prime Minister Churchill. The Charter asserted that the signatory nations wished no aggrandizement, no increase of territory which was against the wishes of the people directly concerned. They respected the right of people to choose their own form of government. They favored equality of economic opportunity for all nations. They hoped to promote fair labor standards, freedom from want and fear, freedom of the seas, and disarmament of aggressor nations. This pact was endorsed (Sept. 24) by 15 governments (9 in exile): Australia, Belgium, Canada, Czechoslovakia, the Free French, Great Britain, Greece, Luxemburg, the Netherlands, New Zealand, Norway, Poland, USSR, Union of South Africa, and Yugoslavia. Eventually all the United Nations signed the Atlantic Charter.

Atomic Age The era introduced by the successful development of the atomic bomb. It is characterized by the possibilities of unlimited power for industrial and military use.

Atomic Energy Commission of the United Nations Created in 1946. It is now part of the Disarmament Commission. Originally its purpose was to control the use of atomic weapons.

Atoms for Peace A program adopted by the United Nations as proposed by President D. D. Eisenhower. It was a plan to make atomic energy available to the nations of the world for peaceful purposes. It was accepted by the U.N. in 1954.

Attlee, Clement Richard (1883-) British statesman. After being admitted to the bar (1905), he became a social worker and a lecturer in the London School of Economics prior to World War I, in which he gained the rank of major. He entered Parliament in 1922 and held posts in the Labor cabinets in 1924 and 1929. In 1935 he succeeded George Lansbury as party leader. In Churchill's war-time coalition cabinet he was lord of the privy seal (1940-42), deputy prime minister (1942-45), dominions secretary (1942-43), and lord president of the council (1943-45). He was prime minister in the Labor government from 1945 to 1951.

Austria, Creation of The Austro-Hungarian Empire was dissolved after World War I into independent states based on ethnic groupings. The Republic of Austria, a grouping of Alpine provinces with a German-speaking population, arose out of this division. The economic unbalance caused by the dissolution of the Empire led to great financial distress in the landlocked republic. Loans were made by Italy, Great Britain, and France of $48,000,000. There were relief credits given between 1919 and 1921 of $100,000,000 by the smaller countries of western Europe. Through the League of Nations Council a loan of $135,000,000 was given (1922) together with a guarantee of her political and economic integrity.

Autarchy In modern usage, a term meaning economic self-sufficiency. The term was used to describe Germany's drive for independence from external sources that could be stopped by a continental blockade.

Authoritarianism
See Communism, Fascism.

Awami League The second largest party in Pakistan. Led by Husain Shahid Suhrawardy. See Moslem League.

Axis, Rome-Berlin Created October 25, 1936. A pact between Germany and Italy which marked the division of Europe into contending groups. The Axis was solidified by an Italo-German treaty of alliance (May 22, 1939). This alliance was later extended (September 27, 1940) to include Japan. (See Anti-Comintern Pact.) Later, Hungary, Romania, Bulgaria, Slovakia, and Croatia adhered to this alliance.

Axis Satellite Nations, Fate of On Dec. 12, 1946 the Council of Foreign Ministers, meeting in New York, completed peace treaties with Italy, Hungary, Bulgaria, Romania, and Finland. On June 5, 1947, the United States Senate ratified all of them except the treaty with Finland (the United States never declared war on Finland).

Italy lost small border regions to France and Yugoslavia, and Trieste (which became a Free Territory under supervision of the Security Council of the U.N.). To Greece, Italy ceded the Dodecanese Islands. The future of Italy's African colonies was to be decided later. (Italy retains a trusteeship over Somaliland. Eritrea has become independent and is incorporated into Ethiopia. Libya has become an independent kingdom.) Italy was to pay reparations to the extent of 360 million dollars to Greece, Ethiopia, Albania, and the USSR. Severe restrictions were placed on future military strength.

Hungary ceded some territory to Czechoslovakia and the eastern half of Transylvania to Romania. Reparations of 300 million dollars were to be paid to the USSR, Czechoslovakia, and Yugoslavia.

Romania lost Bessarabia and Bukovina to the USSR and paid Russia 300 million dollars in reparations.

Bulgaria lost no territory, but was forced to pay reparations to Greece and Yugoslavia.

Finland lost the province of Petsamo to Russia and paid to Russia 300 million dollars.

14

Azaña, Manuel (1880-1940) Spanish statesman. He was a lawyer, author, and teacher in Madrid University. War minister (1931), prime minister (1931-33), president (1936-39). He was a leader of the Republican Left. In February 1939, he fled to France, where he lived until his death.

Azikiwe, Dr. Nnamai (1904-) Nigerian statesman. He leads the dominant political party, the National Council of Nigeria and the Cameroons.

B

Badoglio, Pietro (1871-) Italian field marshal. After serving in the First World War, he was governor of Libya (1929-33). He finished the conquest of Ethiopia (1936). He was made duke of Addis Ababa, viceroy of Ethiopia, and chief of staff of the Italian army (to 1940), he was made premier and negotiated an armistice with the United Nations. He resigned (1944) because of much opposition.

Bagdad Pact (1955) A pact adhered to by Iraq, Turkey, Iran, the United Kingdom, and Pakistan. A defense pact acting as a bulwark against Soviet expansion southward in the Near East. The United States has supported the treaty, and joined a number of its committees. It has never formally joined the pact. All nations of the Near East, with the exception of Israel may join the pact. The pact has been coldly received by the neutralist-minded Arab League.

Balance of Power A system used in Europe balancing groups of nations to prevent any one nation from gaining a position of power. It is now applied to the United States-USSR balance in the "COLD WAR."

Baldwin, Stanley (1867-1947) First Earl Baldwin of Bewdley. British statesman. Active head of iron and steel firm (1892-1916). He entered Parliament in

1908. He was prime minister in Conservative governments in 1923 and 1924-29 and (1935-37) in the National government.

Balfour Declaration (1917) The statement of the British government in a letter from the then foreign secretary A. J. Balfour to Lord Rothschild, British Zionist Federation Chairman, expressing the desire of the government to establish a national home for the Jewish people in Palestine. The state of Israel was founded in Palestine on May 14, 1948.

Balkan Pact (Feb. 9, 1934) A treaty between Turkey, Greece, Romania, and Yugoslavia. It created an alliance like the LITTLE ENTENTE. It was designed to protect the Balkans from the aggression of other countries. Its weakness was the absence of Bulgaria.

Balkanizing Dividing up a geographical region into a number of small countries as was done in the Balkan Peninsula in the late 19th and early 20th centuries. Since the problems that follow division are usually more acute than the ones that precede division "Balkanizing" is a term of reproach, rather than of approbation.

Baltic States, Soviet Annexation of (1940) On Sept. 29, 1939, the day after Germany and Russia partitioned Poland, the USSR signed a pact of mutual assistance with Estonia. Within two weeks the USSR signed similar agreements with Latvia and Lithuania. All three pacts contained promises that the USSR would not interfere with the liberty of the Baltic States. On June 14, 1940, the USSR presented an ultimatum to Lithuania, which charged that Lithuania had violated the pact. On June 16, 1940, similar ultimatums were sent to Estonia and Latvia. Each document demanded the right to have Red troops enter the Baltic States. Thus the Baltic States were occupied by the USSR. Following occupation, the constitutional governments of the Baltic States resigned and were replaced by

16

Russian puppets. After plebiscites, all three countries became republics in the USSR.

Bamboo Curtain   The expression referring to the policy of Communist China in allowing only government-approved communication with the outside world. See Iron Curtain.

Bandaranaike, Solomon West Ridgway Diaz (1909-)   Ceylonese statesman. Elected Prime Minister of Ceylon, in April 1956.

Bandung Conference
See Afro-Asian Conference.

Bank for International Settlements   An international bank chartered in Switzerland in 1930 according to the proposals of the YOUNG PLAN. Its initial authorized capital was $100,000,000 of which $25,000,000 was immediately subscribed. The bank was founded to assist the transfer of international funds (see European Payments Union), to act as trustee for German reparations (see Reparations), and to foster the co-operation of central banks.

Bao Dai   Negotiated with France to create the Democratic Republic of Vietnam (1947), with himself as head of state. Prior to 1945 he was the Emperor of Annam. He was deposed by plebiscite as the head of the state of Vietnam in 1955.

Baruch, Bernard M. (1870-)   Financier. b. New York City. Graduated from City College of N. Y. 1889. Appointed by PRESIDENT WILSON to Advisory Committee of Council of National Defense in 1916. Took charge of raw materials for War Industries Board, serving as chairman, 1918. Served as a member of the drafting committee of the economic section at the Paris Conference. U.S. representative on the Atomic Energy Committee 1946. Author of *Baruch, my Own Story*. See BARUCH PLAN.

Baruch Plan (1946)   A proposal for international atomic energy control submitted in 1946 to the UNITED NA-

TIONS by Bernard Baruch of the United States. The plan recommended international ownership of all mines and plants producing atomic material, and a system of licensing the control and use of such material under international inspection. All atomic weapons were to be destroyed as the inspection and ownership features went into effect. The plan was later widened into the Lilienthal Plan which called for an International Atomic Development Agency to own all power stations and inventions based on atomic power. Both plans were vetoed by the USSR as incompatible with its sovereignty.

Bastogne City in Belgium near St.-Vith which was the object of a German drive attempting to reach and recapture Antwerp. Because of erroneous information given by a Belgian farmer to German advance units the American forces reached Bastogne first. A handful of American paratroopers held the besieged city while swarms of Allied bombers attacked the besiegers paving the way for General Patton's rescue expedition from the south. To a demand for the surrender of Bastogne made by the German general, the American General McAuliffe made his now famous reply, the single word, "Nuts." By December 28, 1944 American tanks rolled into Bastogne and it became an advanced position of the Allied front.

Bataan, Battle of (1942) The struggle by the U.S. forces under General Wainwright to maintain their foothold on the peninsula of Bataan located on the island of Luzon in the Philippines. In the first weeks of the war in the Pacific, the U.S. and the Filipino armies under the command of GENERAL MACARTHUR retreated across Luzon, moving into the peninsula in Jan. 1942. For three months they suffered privations due to lack of food, medicines, and supplies until forced to surrender to the Japanese in April. Previously, General MacArthur had left for Australia, leaving the command in the hands of General Wainwright. Bataan was liberated by U.S. troops in Feb. 1945.

Battle Act A law of Congress passed in 1951. It provided that any nation which shipped war-useful materials to Soviet-dominated countries would automatically lose U.S. aid unless the President determined that the cessation of such aid would hurt the nation's security.

"Battle of Wheat" An attempt by the Fascist government of Italy to increase domestic production of wheat. Prizes for wheat production were contributed by the government, which also encouraged the formation of farm-cooperatives. An educational campaign to improve farm methods was inaugurated. Attempts were made to induce Italians to eat less spaghetti and macaroni. Later the campaign became known as the "Battle of Agriculture" and efforts were made to increase the yield of rice, oats, and corn, as well as wheat.

Beer-Hall Putsch (Nov. 8-11, 1923) An unsuccessful coup against the government organized by LUDENDORFF and HITLER. It took place in Munich. One reason for its failure was that it ran counter to the schemes of a second group of conspirators. Hitler was sentenced to five years in prison for his part in the Putsch. While in prison he wrote "Mein Kampf." He was released after serving less than one year.

Benelux (1947) A tripartite customs union formed by Belgium, the Netherlands, and Luxemburg. Benelux negotiates for the three countries in relation to matters concerning external trade.

Benes, Eduard (1884-1948) Czechoslovak statesman. Born in Kozlany. A professor of sociology in the University of Prague, he became an exile during WORLD WAR I. He worked with Masaryk for Czechoslovak independence. He was foreign minister (1918-33) and premier as well (1921-22). He was president (1935-38). He resigned the presidency in 1938 and went into exile.

In 1939 he became president-in exile, living first in France and later in England. In 1945 he returned to Czechoslovakia and was reelected president in 1946. After the communist coup of 1948 he was president in name only. He resigned, to die a few months later.

Ben-Gurion, David (1886-) Israeli leader and statesman. He was born in Plonsk, Poland. He studied law at the University of Istanbul. After settling in Palestine he was ousted for promoting Zionism. He became an exponent of Zionism for the General Council of the Zionist Organization. Coming back to Palestine, he was made Secretary-General of Histadruth, the Jewish Labor Organization, 1921-1935. He was the leader of the underground Jewish army, Haganah (later to become the Israeli army). As the leader of the Mapai party, he became Prime Minister of Israel 1949-53, 1955-. He is a moderate socialist.

Berchtold, Count Leopold von (1863-1942) Austrian statesman. Ambassador to St. Petersburg (1907-11). Foreign minister (1912-15). He prepared the ultimatum to Serbia (1914), which precipitated World War I. He is one of the leaders who must assume responsibility for beginning the war.

Berlin Airlift (1948-1949) A concerted attempt by the U.S. Air Force to fly food and other supplies into Berlin in 1948 and 1949 in an effort to overcome the Soviet blockade of that city. On April 1, 1948 the Soviet military government in Berlin began a land blockade of the allied areas of that city by refusing to permit American and British supply trains to pass through their zone. By Sept. 30, 1949, when the blockade of the Allied areas ended, the United States airforce had flown over two million tons of food and coal into western Berlin.

Bernadotte, Count Folke (1895-1948) b. Stockholm, Educated at Karlberg Military School. Was Commander of the Swedish pavilion at the New York

World's Fair, 1939-40. Served as President of the Swedish Boy Scouts and director of Swedish Red Cross. He effected the exchange of British and German prisoners in World War II. He also served as intermediary between Himmler and the Allies in the peace overtures of 1945. In 1948 he became U.N. mediator in Palestine, where, as a result of internecine fighting he was assassinated in the late summer of 1948 by members of the outlawed Jewish terrorist organization—the Stern gang.

Bessarabia, Annexation of by the USSR (June 27, 1940) On June 26, 1940, the USSR informed Romania that "justice" demanded the return to Russia of Bessarabia, a region which Romania annexed from Russia in 1919. In addition, northern Bukovina was also to be ceded because of the "community of historic interest" between that region and Russia. King Carol II appealed to Berlin and Rome for advice. He was evidently told to accede to the demand. On the next day Russian troops occupied both regions. They have since become the Moldavian Republic, one of the 16 republics in the USSR.

Bethmann-Hollweg, Theobald von (1856-1921) German statesman. Chancellor of the German Empire (1909-17). He advocated greater autonomy for Alsace-Lorraine and other reforms. He referred to Belgian neutrality treaty as a "scrap of paper." Forced out of office by Hindenburg and Ludendorff (1917).

Bevan, Aneurin (1897-) British Labor politician. A coal miner and trade union leader, he became minister of health in 1945 and administered the program of socialized medicine instituted by the Labor government.

Bevin, Ernest (1881-1951) British Labor leader and statesman. After working as a longshoreman, he became a trade union organizer. He unified 32 separate unions into the Transport and General Workers' Union (1921). In the Churchill war coalition cabinet (1940-

45) he held the post of Minister of Labor and National Service. In the Attlee government he was Foreign Secretary (1945-51). He was strongly opposed to the Soviet Union.

Big Five The name applied to President WILSON, Prime Minister LLOYD GEORGE, Premier CLEMENCEAU, Premier ORLANDO, and Premier Saionji at the VERSAILLES CONFERENCE. The term is also applied to President F. D. ROOSEVELT, Prime Minister CHURCHILL, Premier DE GAULLE, Premier STALIN, and Generalissimo CHIANG KAI-SHEK, during and after World War II. After World War II President TRUMAN and Prime Minister ATTLEE succeeded to executive leadership in the United States and Great Britain. The term "Big Four," refers to the same groupings with the exclusion of Saionji in the first group, and the exclusion of De Gaulle in the second group.

Big Three A term mainly applied to the Allied leaders in World War II, President ROOSEVELT, Premier STALIN, and Prime Minister CHURCHILL.

Bizonia Britain and the U.S. cooperated so well in the handling of their zones of occupation in Germany that on January 1, 1947, the two zones were linked together to form "Bizonia." After some delay, France agreed, early in 1948, to join her zone with that of Bizonia.

Black and Tans English "Auxiliaries" sent over to reinforce the Irish police in the troubled times following the end of World War I. They were so called because their uniform consisted of a khaki outfit with black bands on hat and arm.

Black Hand A secret, nationalistic Serbian society (also called the Union of Death) formed in 1911, and pledged to join Serbia and the other Serb-speaking peoples in a union. Its membership throughout the Balkans was drawn from the army, government, police, University of Belgrade and many members of the less bloodthirsty Narodna Odbrana. It was a member

of the Black Hand who fired the fatal shot at SARA-
JEVO in June, 1914.

"Blank Check" On July 5 and 6, 1914, Germany promised to support Austria-Hungary without qualification
in its quarrel with Serbia over the assassination of
Archduke FRANCIS FERDINAND. This act provided the
impetus which induced Austria-Hungary to issue the
ultimatum which began World War I.

Bloc The usual arrangement in the French Assembly for
forming a majority government. A group of minority
parties of similar interests vote together to form the
government. Examples are the National Bloc in 1919,
and the Popular Front before World War II.

Blockade of Germany In both the First and Second
World Wars, Great Britain using her control of the
seas, attempted to blockade Germany on the continent. This was to keep her from external sources of
trade. Germany, prior to the Second World War, tried
to create an AUTARCHY so as to limit the effect of any
blockade.

Blood Purge, Nazi (June 30, 1934) Early in 1934 there
was serious unrest in the Nazi ranks. Many of the SA
(storm troops) had once been communists and re-
sented the fact that the socialist planks in the Nazi
program had not been carried out. Brown Shirt leader,
Rohm, also wanted a large number of the SA to be
incorporated into the regular army. This, Hitler and
the generals opposed. The malcontents plotted to
overthrow the government. The plot was discovered
and its leaders were "purged," that is, assassinated.
The purge was carried out by the SS (Elite Guards).
It is not known how many people perished. Among
the prominent persons who were killed were Rohm,
former chancellor von Schleicher and his wife, the
leader of Catholic Action, and three of von Papen's
assistants. Soon after the purge the size of the SA

23

was drastically reduced, and the members were largely disarmed.

Blum, Léon (1872-1950) French statesman and writer. He entered politics during the Dreyfus Affair. In 1936, he effected a coalition of Radical Socialists, Socialists, and Communists called the POPULAR FRONT. The Popular Front enacted a kind of New Deal program, proposed nationalizing major industries, and reorganized the Bank of France. Defeated in 1937, Blum served as vice premier (1937-38). He was arrested (1940) by the Vichy government and imprisoned in Austria. After negotiating a credit arrangement with the United States (1946), he again served as premier for two months (1946-47). Author of *Marriage* and *For All Mankind*.

Bogota Conference (1948) This conference, also called the Ninth International Conference of American States, created the ORGANIZATION OF AMERICAN STATES, out of the old PAN AMERICAN UNION. It was held in Bogota, Columbia.

Bolshevism A form of revolutionary socialism developed in Russia and based upon the teachings of KARL MARX. Today it is generally known as communism. The major point of Bolshevism is the dictatorship of the proletariat for the purpose of creating a communistic society. The term came into being in 1903 at the meeting of the Social Democratic party when Lenin's theory of revolution clashed with that of Martov. Lenin's supporters, who outnumbered the others, were called Bolsheviki (majority); the opponents were called Mensheviki (minority). Some of the tenets of Bolshevism are belief in an armed revolution of the proletariat; complete abandonment of the bourgeois liberals; hostility to religion; complete nationalization of means of production; and belief in world revolution.

Bonn Protocol (Nov. 1949) At the Potsdam Conference

(July-Aug. 1945) it was decided that German reparations were to be collected from current assets in the form of factories, machinery, locomotives, and similar capital goods. The bulk of the reparations was to go to the Soviet Union, although 18 other countries, including France, Czechoslovakia, Norway, Albania, India, and Holland, were to have a share. This program was to have been completed by June, 1948, but was extended to July, 1950. As time progressed, it became clear that if many factories in the Western zone of Germany were dismantled, severe shortages would result, which would have to be made up by American aid. Accordingly, the Bonn Protocol was signed between West Germany and the Western Allies under which the dismantling program was halted and plants already dismantled, but not removed from Germany, would remain in the country. Under the original program, 1977 plants were scheduled for dismantling. Actually, only 754 plants were dismantled.

Bonn Republic
See German Federal Republic.

Boris III (1894-1943)   King of Bulgaria (1918-1943).

Bourgeoisie   In Marxian economic theory, the "middle class," supposedly the enemy of the proletariat or working class.

Bourguiba, Habib (1904-)   Tunisian statesman and leader. Prime Minister of Tunisia since the beginning of its independence (April 1956).

Brainwashing   A system of psychological pressure used on United Nations troops that were captured in the KOREAN WAR. They were forced to betray their cause and their national beliefs. The system is also used on political prisoners within the communist countries.

Brandeis, Louis (1856-1941)   Jurist. b. Kentucky. Graduated from Harvard Law School (1879). Opponent of bigness in business and government. Appointed Associate Justice of U.S. Supreme Court in 1916 by President WILSON. He joined Holmes, Cardoza and Stone in a long series of dissenting opinions in Court cases curbing social and economic experimentation by the states. He retired from the Court in 1939.

Brest-Litovsk, Treaty of (March 3, 1918) Between Russia and Germany following the Bolshevik Revolution, Eastern Poland, Lithuania, Estonia, and Livonia were ceded to the Germans. In the south, part of Trans-caucasia was ceded to Turkey. Thus, Russia lost 26% of its population; 27% of its arable land; 32% of average crops; 26% of its railroads; 33% of its factories; 73% of its iron industries; 75% of its coal fields. Germany was forced to renounce this treaty by the TREATY OF VERSAILLES (1919).

Bretton Woods Conference (1944) A meeting of 28 nations at Bretton Woods, New Hampshire, convened for the purpose of establishing the INTERNATIONAL BANK FOR RECONSTRUCTION AND DEVELOPMENT, and the INTERNATIONAL MONETARY FUND.

Briand, Aristide (1862-1932) French statesman. Born in Nantes. Deputy (1902-19). Founded Socialist newspaper L'Humanité (1904) with Jaurès. Prime minister (1909-11). Head of coalition government (1915-17). Prime minister (1921-22). French representative at the Washington Conference (1922). Minister of foreign affairs (1925-32). Awarded Nobel Peace Prize (1926) with GUSTAV STRESEMANN. With Kellogg, developed the KELLOGG-BRIAND PEACE PACT (1927-28) (also known as the Pact of Paris).

British Caribbean Federation A union of the thirteen islands and numberless islets belonging to the British in the Caribbean sea which aspire to independence and nationhood. In their first election as a federation they selected 45 members for a House of Representatives to sit at the designated capital, Port of Spain, Trinidad.

British Commonwealth The grouping of nations of what

was formerly the British Empire. It is made up of the United Kingdom, India, Canada, Australia, Ceylon, Union of South Africa, Pakistan, and New Zealand. Its formal head is the Queen of the United Kingdom. There are certain intra-Commonwealth economic advantages for the members.

British Union of Fascists This black-shirted group was organized by Sir Oswald Mosley in 1932. It advocated greater development of the home market, the establishment of a national council of industry, and a social and moral rejuvenation. After 1934, the British Fascists had numerous clashes with the police. In 1937 the Public Order Act, aimed at the Mosley group, forbade the wearing of political uniforms and the formation of semi-military organizations. Mosley was imprisoned during the war and his organization disbanded.

Brussels Treaty Organization (March 1948) A defense treaty organization originally signed by the United Kingdom, the Netherlands, Luxemburg, Belgium, and France. It was later expanded to include the German Federal Republic and Italy, in May 1955 (see Western European Union).

Bryan, William Jennings (1860-1925) Orator and political leader. b. Salem, Illinois. Graduated from Illinois college (1881) and from Union College of Law in Chicago (1883). Practiced in Lincoln, Nebraska where he became active in Democratic politics. Member of House of Representatives in 1891-1895, where he joined the silver bloc. His "Cross of Gold" speech (1896) won him the presidential nomination at the Chicago Democratic convention. Although he campaigned vigorously and had the support of Populists, Democrats and Silver Republicans he lost to McKinley by 600,000 votes. Unsuccessful presidential candidate for the Democrats in 1900, 1908. Secretary of State in Wilson's cabinet (1913-5). Advocated strict neutrality

27

after outbreak of World War I. A fundamentalist in religion, in 1925 he prosecuted John Scopes in Dayton, Tennessee for teaching evolution in public schools.

Buenos Aires Conference (1936) A Pan-American conference personally attended by F. D. Roosevelt. Formally called the Inter-American Conference for the Maintenance of Peace, the meeting provided for the mutual consultation of the Latin American nations on all matters affecting hemispheric peace. The Conference adopted a neutrality convention obligating its members to take a common joint attitude as neutrals in the event of an outbreak of hostilities between any two of them.

Bulganin, Nikolai Alexandrovitch (1895-) Soviet statesman. A member of the communist party at the time of the Bolshevik revolution. Chairman of the Moscow Soviet (1931). Member of the Central Committee of the Communist Party (1935). Lieutenant General and Marshal in the Russian Army in World War II. Chairman of the Council of Ministers (1955-1958). Chairman of the Moscow Bank (1958-   ).

Bulge, Battle of the A strong counter attack in the Ardennes by 15 German divisions under General Von Rundstedt, begun on Dec. 16, 1944. Within five days the 1st U.S. Army had been driven out of Germany by the enemy push which succeeded in penetrating 50 miles into the American lines. Reinforced by General Patton's 3rd Army on Dec. 21st, the Americans stemmed the Nazi drive by Christmas. The counter offensive from that day succeeded in wiping out the bulge by Jan. 31, 1945. Estimated U.S. losses were 59,000 as compared with the German casualties of 220,000 dead, wounded, and prisoners. This marked the last German offensive effort in World War II.

Bunche, Ralph Johnson (1904-) American Negro statesman. He was instrumental in restoring peace in the

28

Near East after the ARAB-ISRAELI WAR (1948-49), as a special mediator for the UNITED NATIONS.

Burma, Creation of the Union of (1948) Prior to World War II, a colony of Great Britain, administered as a part of India. With the Japanese occupation a supposedly independent Burmese government was set up. It was reoccupied by Great Britain after the war. In 1948 the Union of Burma was set up comprising Burma, the Shan State, the Karenni State, and Chin Special Division. It is not a member of the British Commonwealth.

Byelorussia, Annexation of An ethnic area containing "white Russians." It was taken from the USSR by Poland in 1920. It was reannexed by the USSR in 1939 as a result of the German-Soviet partition of Poland. It is now a republic within the USSR.

Byrnes, James F. (1879-) Statesman. Public school education. Admitted to bar, 1903. U.S. Senator from South Carolina, 1931-41. Justice in U.S. Supreme Court 1941-2, when he resigned to become Director of Economic Stabilization and War Mobilization, 1943-5. Served as Secretary of State from 1945-7 under President TRUMAN. Democratic governor of South Carolina for term 1951-5.

C

Cairo Conference (1943) A meeting of President F. D. Roosevelt, Prime Minister Winston Churchill, and Premier Chiang Kai-Shek in Nov. 1943. It was called for the purpose of formulating a Far Eastern program. The declaration issued stated that, following Allied victory, Japan would lose all the islands in the Pacific seized since 1914, and that all the territories stolen from China (Manchuria, Formosa, and the Pescadores) would be restored to the Republic of China. Agreement was reached that Korea would become a free and independent state.

Camelot du Roi French rightist party which in the 1920's and '30's advocated a monarchial revival and clericalism.

Canadian-American Defense Conference (1940) President F. D. Roosevelt and Prime Minister Mackenzie King of Canada met Aug. 18, 1940 in Ogdensburg, New York, to discuss joint defense. At this meeting it was decided to pool American and Canadian resources for the defense of the North American continent.

Canal Waters Dispute A controversy between India and Pakistan (since their independence) over the canals and rivers flowing from India into West Pakistan. These waterways are vital for commerce. The situation had caused mutual tension, and has not yet been settled permanently.

Capitalism The economic system based on the investment of capital funds for private profit. Under this system the means of production are privately owned. Production of goods and services is done for the market. "Pure" capitalism is characterized by the individual entrepreneur and a market economy, with no government interference. Modern "capitalist" states have some degree of public control and ownership of the means of production. (See Socialism, Communism).

Caporetto Campaign (Oct. 24-Dec. 26, 1917) German-Austrian troops attacked the Italians during a heavy fog. The Italian troops broke at once. They fell back on the Piave River, where, with French and British support, they made an effective stand. The troops of the Central Powers, outrunning their supplies, were forced to slow down. Italian General Cadorna was replaced by General Diaz, who established a strong defensive position. The Italians lost 300,000 prisoners.

Caribbean Policy The term expressing the interest of the U.S. and its program of political control in the islands and mainland of the Caribbean Sea. In the WILSON, HARDING, COOLIDGE, and HOOVER administrations repeated military interventions were conducted in those nations of the Caribbean. It was not until the adoption of the "GOOD NEIGHBOR" policy of President F. D. ROOSEVELT that the last American forces were withdrawn.

Carol II (1893-1953) King of Romania (1930-40). When crown prince he formed a liaison with Magda Lupescu. For this he was forced to renounce his rights to the throne and go into exile (1925). When his father, Ferdinand, died in 1927, Michael, became king. Carol returned to Romania (1930) and had himself declared king. His reign was stormy. He was deposed (1940) by ANTONESCU and the IRON GUARD. He lived in exile thereafter.

Casablanca Conference (Jan. 14-24, 1943) A meeting between President Roosevelt and Prime Minister Churchill and their principal military and political leaders at Casablanca, Morocco in Jan., 1943. The meeting was convened for the purpose of planning the succeeding stages of military strategy following the North African invasion of Nov. 1942. From this conference came the demand for "unconditional surrender" of the Axis powers in World War II.

Castro, Fidel Cuban rebel leader in open opposition to the regime of Cuban President Fulgencio Batista.

Central Powers, the Four countries, headed by Germany, which fought against 23 Allied countries during World War I.

31

Country	Date of Entrance into War
Austria-Hungary	July, 1914
Germany	August, 1914
Turkey	October, 1914
Bulgaria	October, 1915

Ceylon, Independence of Formerly a colony of the United Kingdom, Ceylon achieved independence and dominion status by the Ceylon Independence Act of the British Parliament (1947).

Chaco War A series of wars between Bolivia and Paraguay over possession of the Gran Chaco region. On Dec. 6, 1928 military skirmishes broke out and diplomatic relations between these nations were severed. An arbitration treaty of the PAN-AMERICAN CONFERENCE was prepared on Aug. 31, 1929 but rejected by both governments. A temporary truce was negotiated on April 4, 1930 after a year's continued battles. Major fighting was resumed in 1932 despite the efforts of the LEAGUE OF NATIONS and the Pan-American Union to mediate the dispute. Paraguay succeeded in capturing the greater part of the Chaco but failed in attempts to occupy Bolivia proper. On June 14, 1935 Bolivia and Paraguay concluded a truce at the insistence of the U.S. and five South American Republics. A final peace treaty was negotiated on Aug. 21, 1936 on the basis of an arbitration award handed down by the U.S. and the Latin American Governments. By its terms 30,000 sq. miles of the Gran Chaco region were given to Bolivia and 70,000 sq. miles to Paraguay, but Bolivia was furnished with an outlet to the sea through the Paraguay River.

Chamberlain, Sir Austen (1863-1937) British statesman. Son of Joseph Chamberlain and half-brother of NEVILLE CHAMBERLAIN. Unionist M.P. (1892). Civil lord of the admiralty (1895-1900). Chancellor of the exchequer (1903-06). Secretary of state for India (1915-17). Chancellor of exchequer (1919-21). Conservative leader in Commons and lord of privy seal (1921-23). Foreign secretary (1924-29). Awarded Nobel peace prize jointly with Charles G. Dawes (1925). Attended all meetings of the Council and Assembly of the League of Nations. Supported the KELLOGG-BRIAND PEACE PACT (1928).

Chamberlain, Arthur Neville (1869-1940) British statesman. Son (by second marriage) of Joseph Chamberlain. Lord Mayor of Birmingham (1915-16), Chancellor of Exchequer (1931-37), Minister of Health (1924-29), Prime Minister (1937-40). For the sake of peace, while his country was unprepared, he adopted a policy of appeasement. Criticism of the MUNICH SETTLEMENT and his conduct of the war forced his resignation a few months before his death.

Chapultepec, Act of (March 8, 1945) A regional mutual defense treaty for the nations of the western hemisphere, created by the Inter-American Conference meeting at Mexico City. It was sanctioned by the United Nations as collective self-defense.

Château-Thierry, Battle of An important engagement in World War I in which the U.S. 2nd and 3rd Divisions, assisted by French forces, broke the German advance on June 4, 1918. In this battle 85,000 American troops prevented the Germans from crossing the Marne and continuing their march on Paris. On June 5th the marines of the 2nd Division opened a six day battle against enemy forces entrenched in nearby Belleau Wood. By June 11th the Germans had been ejected. Mopping up the surrounding area in the next two weeks, the U.S. Army had succeeded in clearing the area by June 25th. American casualties totalled 9,500.

Cheka (Extraordinary Commission for the Suppression of

Counter-Revolution) Created on Dec. 20, 1917, by the Russian Soviets to suppress counter-revolution. It was often called "The Red Terror."

Chetniks Yugoslav guerrillas who, under the leadership of General Mikhailovich, carried on a continuously successful warfare against the Nazi conquerors of their country.

Chiang Kai-Shek (1886-) Chinese military leader and statesman. Chief of Staff under Sun Yat Sen in Chinese revolutionary army (1924). Head of Chinese government (1925). Fought Chinese Communists until the Japanese invasion of China. He led the Nationalist forces against the Japanese until 1945. After 1945 he fought a losing Civil war with the Chinese Communists. In 1948 he moved the Nationalist government to Formosa. He is now supported with his army on Formosa with American aid.

China, Renunciation of Extraterritorial Rights in In 1928 the Chinese Nationalist government passed a new criminal code and asked all nations with interests in China to renounce their extraterritorial rights. In 1928, Portugal, Denmark, Belgium, and Italy renounced these rights. The U.S. and the United Kingdom, during World War II compensated China for being neglected by Allied aid, by abrogating extraterritoriality for American and British nationals (1943).

China White Paper (1949) A document issued by the State Department of the U.S. on Aug. 5, 1949 absolving the U.S. from responsibility for the success of the Chinese Communists against the nationalist regime of CHIANG KAI-SHEK. In Nov. 1945 President TRUMAN had appointed General Marshall as his special envoy to China for the purpose of investigating the possibilities of creating a strong, united, and democratic China. The President declared that the U.S. favored the termination of one-party government and the establishment of a coalition government of the two major political forces in China. This hope was repeated by the foreign ministers of the U.S., U.K., and the Soviet Union on Dec. 27, 1945. In Feb. 1946 General Marshall's headquarters in China declared that an agreement had been reached. The opposition of the nationalist regime to admit Communists into a coalition government prevented the agreement from being carried out. In the summer of 1946 Marshall returned to China in the attempt to develop new conditions of agreement, but announced in Aug. that a settlement was impossible. In Jan. 1947 he returned to the U.S. and issued a statement in which he denounced the "dominant group of reactionaries" in the national government who had prohibited the formation of a genuine coalition government. He attacked the propaganda of the Chinese Communist party as harmful. Subsequently the U.S. dissolved its special agencies and withdrew all American troops from China. The White Paper was the justification of U.S. policies in this conflict.

Chinese-Japanese Undeclared War (1937-1945) A number of incidents precipitated a Japanese invasion of Shanghai on Aug. 8, 1937. The Japanese continued invading the mainland of China penetrating deeply. The Second World War expanded the war, allying China with the Allies. Through clever fighting, the Chinese prevented the Japanese from conquering the entire country. The Japanese preoccupation with fighting in the Pacific, allowed the Chinese to halt the Japanese penetration. The American victories in the Pacific for all intents caused a Chinese victory. The war ended coincident with the end of World War II.

Chou En-Lai (1898-) Chinese Communist revolutionary and statesman. In the People's Republic of China he is Chief of the State Council or Premier and Foreign Minister. He has assumed these posts since 1949.

Christian Democratic Union The coalition party headed by Dr. Konrad Adenauer in Germany, consisted of the former Center party, the Bavarian Catholic party and other non-Marxist socialistic elements outside these two groups. Since the establishment of the West German Federal Republic, this pro-Ally faction has maintained control of the parliament at Bonn and its policy has been guided in its pro-Western course by the astute, diplomatic Dr. ADENAUER.

Christian Socialism This movement arose during the latter part of the 19th century from the growing sense of social responsibility. Many people began to accept the idea that it is society's duty to prevent poverty rather that to relieve it. Many clergymen felt that the capitalistic system was unchristian, since it imposed poverty on the masses while the rich capitalists lived in luxury. When Pope Leo XIII issued his famous encyclical, Rerum Novarum, in 1891, which defended private property as a natural right but condemned social abuses, many European Catholics adopted Christian Socialism. Following this lead, the Catholic Center Party of Germany and the Catholic Party in Belgium, although strongly opposed to Marxism, began to support the Socialist parties to obtain social reform. In England there was a similar movement. British Christian Socialists advocated a return to those principles which had guided the Christian communities in the 1st century.

Churchill, Sir Winston Leonard Spencer (1874-) English statesman, soldier, and author. Educated at Harrow and Sandhurst, he first saw active military service for the Spanish in Cuba in 1895. Thereafter, he served in the Northwest Frontier of India, the Sudan, and the Boer War. He was elected to Parliament as a Conservative in 1900. In 1906 he became a Liberal and was secretary for colonies in the Campbell-Bannerman cabinet (1905-08). President of the Board of Trade (1908-10); home secretary (1910-11), first lord of the admiralty (1911-15). He was discredited by the failure of the Gallipoli Campaign which he sponsored and was forced to resign. He returned to the cabinet as minister of munitions (1917) and secretary of state for war and for air (1918-21). Again as a Conservative, he served as colonial secretary (1921) and chancellor of the exchequer (1924-29). He held no cabinet positions for the next 10 years. In 1939 he was made first lord of the admiralty. In May, 1940, when Chamberlain was forced to resign, Churchill became prime minister. He was Britain's great war prime minister. He, together with Roosevelt and Stalin, were three of the most powerful figures in the world. In 1945, just after victory in Europe, his party was defeated at the polls, and Churchill had to resign. He and his party were returned to power in 1951. Churchill is a prolific writer of books. Among his works are *Marlborough, World Crisis, The Gathering Storm, Their Finest Hour,* and *The Grand Alliance.* He received the Nobel Prize for literature in 1953. He retired as prime minister April 5, 1955 and was succeeded by Anthony Eden.

Chu-Te (1886-) Chinese Communist statesman and soldier. Chinese Communist Commander-in-Chief of the Armed Forces. Vice-Chairman of the Government Council.

Ciano, Count Galeazzo (1903-44) Italian Fascist leader. Mussolini's son-in-law. Minister of propaganda (1934); minister of foreign affairs (1936-43). He supported his father-in-law's expansionist and foreign policy. As the war went against Italy, he wavered. In 1943 he voted to discontinue the Fascist regime. He was later captured by the Germans in north Italy, tried by the Fascist government, and executed by a firing squad.

Civil Disobedience A system of non-cooperation and passive resistance against the government, originated by the American, Thoreau in his writings. In contemporary history its most spectacular use was by GANDHI and his followers in India against the British colonial government.

Clemenceau, Georges (1841-1929) French statesman. "The Tiger." Correspondent in the United States after the Civil War (1866). Member of the Chamber of Deputies (1871, 1876-93). Senator (from 1902). Premier (1906-09). Again premier (1917-1920) when he led France through a critical period of World War I. He represented France at the Versailles Peace Conference (1919). He retired to private life in 1920.

"Cold War" The popular name applied to the deterioration of American-Soviet relations after 1946. In the absence of outright warfare a series of diplomatic controversies developed to a point of open political hostility, fed by the mutual propaganda attacks of these nations' governments and publicity media. The more outstanding controversies included the TRUMAN DOCTRINE, MARSHALL PLAN, NORTH ATLANTIC TREATY, MUTUAL SECURITY PROGRAM, BERLIN BLOCKADE, BERLIN AIRLIFT, JAPANESE PEACE TREATY, KOREAN WAR, and WARSAW PACT, extension of Soviet power in central and eastern Europe, assumption of power by the Chinese Communists and the division and OCCUPATION OF GERMANY.

Collective Security A plan among the nations to take concerted action against military aggression in order to defend international peace and security. From time to time such plans have been embodied in international agreements and in the work of world organizations such as the LEAGUE OF NATIONS, the UNITED NATIONS, and the HAGUE TRIBUNAL. Among the international agreements providing for collective security have been the arbitration treaties drafted at the Hague Tribunal, the KELLOGG-BRIAND PEACE PACT, and the NORTH ATLANTIC TREATY.

Collectivism A term indicative of political and economic systems that replace cooperation for competition as the basic mode of action.

Colombo Plan (1950) At the British Commonwealth meeting in Colombo, Ceylon, an economic development system was set up to develop the resources of Malaya, Cambodia, Singapore, Vietnam, Laos, Nepal, Thailand, Ceylon, and India. It was to be financed by the International (World) Bank, the U.S., and the leading Commonwealth countries.

Cominform (Communist Information Bureau) An organization which has replaced the Comintern (q.v.), which was abandoned in May, 1943. The Comintern was revived in this new form, following a secret meeting in Poland in 1947. The Cominform was created ostensibly to issue information and to direct propaganda activities. Actually it coordinates the political, economic, cultural, and military affairs in Communist Europe. Its influence is manifest in Italy, France, and even the United States. Its headquarters were located originally in Belgrade. After the defection of Tito, the Cominform headquarters were moved to Bucharest.

Comintern
See Internationales.

Commission on Human Rights In 1946, ECOSOC established a Commission on Human Rights, which prepared a Universal Declaration of Human Rights that was accepted by the General Assembly of the United Nations on Dec. 10, 1948. The Declaration contains 30 articles which deal with individual and personal rights; rights of relationship; economic, social, and cultural rights. It also sets forth conditions under which human rights can be attained.

Communism A social philosophy or a system of social organization based upon the principle of the public

39

ownership of the material instruments of production and economic service, associated with doctrines as to the means by which such a system is to be established and maintained. In its fundamental philosophy, communism is practically identical with socialism (q.v.). Like socialism, it derives much of its support and its theoretical formulation from the works of Karl Marx and Friedrich Engels, although it has given its own special emphasis to certain stereotypes and slogans, such as the "dictatorship of the proletariat." Communism differs from socialism in its repudiation of the philosophy of gradualism and its insistence that slow, piecemeal measures can never be adequate to introduce the new type of society. It may even go so far as to deny the possibility of introducing a collectivized economy by constitutional means, even in states where political democracy exists. Consequently, it is committed to the justifiability, and quite probably the necessity, of forcible or even violent means of breaking down the capitalistic system and introducing the new order. The second important divergence of communism from socialism has to do with the system of compensation of the worker. Both agree that "ownership income" must disappear and only "doership income" remain. But while socialism is content to allow incomes to be adjusted on the basis of personal ability or social service competitively appraised within the collective system, communism would eliminate even the competition of individual quality. The familiar communist slogan, "From each according to his ability and to each according to his need" seems to contest the field with the doctrine of equal pay for all workers. Like socialism, communism is primarily an economic, rather than a political, system. The political implications which seem to infuse communism even more strongly than socialism probably stem from the doctrine, mentioned above, that communism cannot be achieved through the authorized use of political methods even in state systems that have a free electorate. There is no adequate ground, in communist theory or practice, for the assumption that communism is committed to the overthrow of government in general, or of any particular government. No doubt communists would endorse the doctrine that any people whose government has become tyrannical, oppressive, or unresponsive to the popular will, and which cannot be displaced by peaceful means, can be legitimately ousted by forcible means. But in this communists do not differ from any other school which accepts the doctrine of the occasional necessity and justifiability of revolution. It was in keeping with this doctrine that the Union of Soviet Socialist Republics was established in 1917, and the United States of America in 1776. In this connection, it may be noted that communism, in certain periods of its development at least, has been more concerned with world revolution than has socialism. The Union of Soviet Socialist Republics, while unquestionably instituted as the result of communist agitation and in the spirit of communism, is not at present a communistic society. Its own leaders proclaim this fact emphatically, and insist that while they may have a communistic objective in mind, they are still a long way from it, and are at present in the socialist phase. This contention is supported by the great differences in personal incomes that prevail today in the Soviet Union. This country is very far from being a classless society in so far as questions of status, levels of living, and recognition are concerned. In the United States, communism has had a somewhat checkered career. It has existed mainly as a philosophy, never having been established as an economic system on a sufficiently large scale to be significant. There have been several groups using the name and claiming to be the authentic representatives of the doctrine. The Communist Party, as far as any one group can lay exclusive claim to that title, is

41

numerically a very small body. As a group, probably as a result of the vigorous opposition of its opponents, it has a social potential far out of proportion to its numerical strength or to the social potential of its individual members. Before the relative standardization of the concept which followed the work of Marx and Engels, communism frequently had a vaguer but more inclusive connotation. It was considered to involve the common ownership, not only of the material means of production, but of all material instruments, including consumption goods. On account of the strong property implications of the marriage institution, this doctrine frequently led to sweeping modifications in the mores of marriage and the family, involving at least the theoretical implications of communal sex relations. It was on this rock, perhaps as much as any other, that some of the early adventures of Utopian communism eventually foundered. One of the oldest records of a group with definitely communistic features relates to the early Christian church, of which it is said: "Neither said any of them aught of the things which he possessed was his own; but they had all things in common."

Communist Party of the USSR The only party permitted in the USSR. It operates through "cells" which are located in every activity where decisions are made. Its activities are controlled through a Central Committee, which, in turn, is dominated by the Politburo. Membership in the party is severely limited. Each applicant must pass a rigorous trial period and must justify his membership periodically. He must at all times conform to the "party line."

Concentration Camp A place of internment for political prisoners. They are usually held without normal legal processes.

Congress of Oppressed Austrian Nationalities (April 10, 1918) Czech, Yugoslav, Polish and Romanian representatives met in Rome and declared the right of self-determination. They denounced the Hapsburg government for its opposition to the free development of nations. They called upon all fellow nationals to fight against Austria-Hungary. Following this declaration, the independence of Czechoslovakia was recognized by Italy and France on June 30, by Great Britain on Aug. 13, and by the United States on Sept. 3.

Congress Party

See Indian National Congress.

Conscription Compulsory military service. First introduced into the United States during the Civil War as a result of the failure of President Lincoln's call for volunteers. Subsequently employed during World War I and World War II. The first peace-time military conscription law passed by Congress was the Burke-Wadsworth Act of 1940. Conscription was continued following the conclusion of World War II. With the exceptions noted above the United States has always raised its military forces by volunteer enlistments.

Conservative Party, the British Following the enactment of the Reform Bill of 1832, many English Tories rallied around the new standard of "Conservatism," which was erected by Sir Robert Peel. Peel accepted the principles of the Reform Bill, but wished in the future to proceed in a conservative manner. This party has remained a dominant force in England ever since.

Containment A series of steps, military and otherwise, which were designed (since 1947) to check Russian expansion. The United States has been the prime mover in developing this policy and has financed the major part of it.

Contractual Agreement (1952) Since there are deep differences between the Western Powers and the USSR, it has been impossible to conclude a treaty of peace with Germany. In June, 1952, a so-called Contractual

Agreement was drawn up between France, the United States, Great Britain, and the Bonn government to end the war between them and to give West Germany virtual sovereign powers.

Coolidge, John Calvin (1872-1933) Thirtieth President of the United States. b. Plymouth, Vermont. Graduated, Amherst College (1895); studied law and practiced in Northhampton, Massachusetts; mayor of Northhampton (1910-11); elected to Massachusetts state senate (1912-15); president (1914-15); lieutenant governor of Massachusetts (1916-18); governor (1919-20); gained national reputation through his handling of the Boston Police Strike; became Vice-President of the United States (March 4, 1921-August 2, 1923); succeeded to the presidency on the death of HARDING and took the oath of office (August 3, 1923); elected (1924) President of the United States and served until 1928. His years in office were uneventful, but he was popular because of the nation's prosperity. He backed Hoover for President in 1928, not caring to run for office again.

Coral Sea, Battle of An unusual naval-air battle of World War II in which the waterborne air fleets of the United States and Japan attacked each other's navies. The battle was fought in May, 1942, and was the first engagement fought entirely by naval planes from ships that had neither sight nor range of each other. American casualties were 66 planes and 543 men. The Japanese were estimated to have lost 80 planes and 900 men.

Cordon Sanitaire A French policy of the 1920's and 30's to contain Communist Russia. This was done by strengthening the Baltic States, Poland, and Romania.

Corporate State, Italian Before 1914 there developed in Italy the doctrine of syndicalism, which advocated the abolition of political government in favor of government by economic groups. Under the leadership of

44

Edmondo Rossini, the syndicalists united with the Fascists in the struggle against communism. Since by 1926 the syndicalists numbered 2½ million, Mussolini determined to control them. By the Law of 1926, 13 confederated Fascist syndicates (6 of employers, 6 of employees, and 1 of intellectuals) were given legal status. The syndicates acquired the sole right to prepare collective contracts. Strikes and lockouts were forbidden. Sixteen labor courts, from which there was no appeal, were set up. In 1928 a law was passed which made Italy the first Western state to have a national legislature representing economic groups. Membership in the Chamber of Deputies was fixed at 400. The 13 syndicates nominated 800 candidates for this body and the charitable and cultural institutions selected 200 more. From this list of 1,000 names, the Fascist Grand Council chose 400 nominees. Voters were required to vote "Yes" or "No" for the entire 400. In 1934 the Italian Government created 22 new corporations, each of which represented the state, capital, and labor. Three functions were assigned to the corporations: to advise the government; settle labor disputes; and regulate production, distribution, and prices. After several years of further study, the Fascist Grand Council recommended (1938) that the Chamber of Deputies be replaced by a Chamber of Fasces and Corporations. This house was composed of 700, representing the state, the Fascist Party, and the 22 corporations. All were to be appointed by the Head of State (Mussolini). This body first met in March, 1939. Thus national elections were abolished.

Corregidor Island An island in the Philippines off the southern tip of the peninsula of Bataan on Luzon. It was the scene of the last defense of the combined American-Filipino army in the opening months of the War in the Pacific. After surrendering Bataan on April 9, 1942, the army under the command of General Wainwright established its position on Corregidor, holding out until compelled to surrender on May 6th. Corregidor was recaptured from the Japanese in February 1945.

Coty, René Jules Gustave (1882-) French statesman. Elected President of France in 1953.

Council of Europe A consultative body composed of a Committee of Foreign Ministers, and a Consultative Assembly of government representatives. Its members are: France, Denmark, Belgium, Italy, Luxemburg, Ireland, the Netherlands, the United Kingdom, Norway, Sweden, Turkey, Austria, West Germany, Greece and Iceland. Created in 1949.

Council of Foreign Ministers A council of the foreign ministers of the United States, Great Britain, the Soviet Union, France, and China which was established by agreement at the POTSDAM CONFERENCE. The Council was created for the purpose of drafting the peace settlement with the defeated AXIS POWERS. It held its first session in London on September 11, 1945, but adjourned on October 2nd without success. The second meeting was held in December, 1945 in Moscow, but again ended in disagreement over the procedure on treaty drafting. In April, 1946 the Council of Foreign Ministers convened in Paris to draw up peace treaties for all the Axis Powers, except Germany and Japan, and adjourned after issuing a call for a peace conference to meet in Paris in July. The next meeting was held in November-December in New York City and produced peace treaties for Finland, Italy, Hungary, Romania, and Bulgaria. A seven-week conference in Moscow in March, 1947 failed in an attempt to prepare peace terms for Germany and Austria. A second meeting in London on November 25th for the purpose of preparing peace treaties for Germany and Austria again failed because of basic differences between the United States and the Soviet

46

Union. In May and June, 1949 a meeting of the Council of Foreign Ministers in Paris failed to agree on terms of German unification, the result leading to a conference in New York on September 19, 1950 of the foreign ministers of the United States, Great Britain, and France in which agreement was reached to end the state of war with Germany. On March 5, 1951 a conference of the deputy ministers of these nations and the Soviet Union was called for the discussion of international tensions with emphasis on treaties for Germany and Austria, reduction of armed forces, demilitarization of Germany, and re-establishment of German unity. The conference was adjourned on June 21st without success.

Council of Ten Also known as the Supreme Council. It was a committee at the VERSAILLES PEACE CONFERENCE in 1919 consisting of two delegates from each of the BIG FIVE, the United States, Great Britain, France, Italy, and Japan. This group was the core of the Conference, which decided the basic issues of the Treaty.

Cripps, Sir Stafford (1889-1952) British statesman. Brilliant lawyer. Knighted in 1930. A left-wing Labor leader, he was solicitor general (1930-31), but was expelled from the party for being too pro-Communist. When Churchill became prime minister (1940), he made Cripps ambassador to the USSR (1940) and later (1942) lord of the privy seal. In 1942 Cripps was sent to India with a plan for self-government, which India rejected. Upon his return to England he was placed in charge of aircraft production (to 1945). In the Labor Ministry, Cripps (now reinstated in the party) was first (1945) president of the Board of Trade and later (1947) Chancellor of the Exchequer. He was virtually in charge of all of Britain's economy. He carried through the Labor Party's schemes for nationalization of certain industries. He also inaugurated the "austerity" program of food rationing.

Croix de Feu A French fascist association of war veterans during the 1930's. It was led by Colonel François de la Rocque.

Curzon, George Nathaniel, first Marquess Curzon of Kedleston (1859-1925) British statesman. Undersecretary of state for India (1891-92), undersecretary of foreign affairs (1895-98). As Viceroy of India (1899-1905) he strengthened the northwest border defenses and promoted higher education. Lord of the privy seal (1915-16), foreign secretary (1919-24). He presided over the Lausanne Conference (1922-23) and paved the way for the Dawes Plan. During the Paris Peace Conference (1919) he prepared what is since known as the Curzon Line to divide Polish and Russian territory.

Curzon Line (1919) A line for the eastern boundary of Poland which was suggested at the Versailles Conference (q.v.) by Lord Curzon (q.v.). It ran somewhat east of north, from a point on the Carpathians slightly west of where they are intersected by the 23° meridian to a point on the East Prussian frontier northwest of Suwalki. The present boundary between Poland and the USSR follows this line fairly closely.

Czechoslovakia, Annihilation of (March 10-16, 1939) After the Munich Agreement (q.v.), a quarrel arose between Prague and Mgr. Tiso, the premier of Slovakia. This dispute was inspired by the Germans to give them the excuse to interfere further in Czech affairs. The latter appealed to Hitler for help. Hitler's answer was to declare (March 15) Bohemia and Moravia a German protectorate. It was promptly occupied by German troops and von Neurath was made "protector." On March 16, Tiso put Slovakia under German protection.

D

Daladier, Édouard (1884-) French politician. After World War I he was a frequent member of various cabinets. Premier (1933, 1933-34, 1938-40). He was premier during the Stavinsky riots (1934). As premier of France he signed the Munich Agreement (1938) (q.v.). Arrested by Vichy (1940), he was interned in Austria until 1945. He reentered politics in 1946. He is a Radical Socialist.

D'Annunzio, Gabriele (1863-1938) Italian poet, novelist, dramatist, journalist, airman. Born in Pescara. Author of *Il Piacere, L'Innocente, Trionfo della Merte, Il Fuoco, La Citta Morte, La Gioconda, Le Martyre de St. Sebastian.* Grace and affectation characterized his style. He advocated war against Austria, served, and was wounded (1916). In 1919, he organized a black-shirted group of *Arditi* and captured Fiume. He was a staunch supporter of Mussolini.

Danzig Free city and district on the Baltic Sea, formerly part of the German Empire and one of its principal ports. Danzig was nominally under the control of the League of Nations, by which a High Commissioner was appointed to govern the city. With the rise of the Nazis in Germany, agitation developed to have Danzig reincorporated in the Reich. On Aug. 29, 1939, Hitler called upon Poland to sign away all of its rights to Danzig (Danzig's foreign interests were entrusted to Poland, with whom it had a customs union). On Sept. 1, 1939, Germany invaded Poland and the Second World War began. At the end of the war, Danzig was incorporated into Poland.

"date which will live in infamy, a" The quotation from the address to Congress by President F. D. ROOSEVELT on December 8, 1941. Coming a day after the Japanese attack on PEARL HARBOR the President denounced the "unprovoked and dastardly attack" and referred to December 7, 1941 as "a day which will live in infamy." He called upon Congress to declare war on Japan.

Dawes Plan (1924-29) A plan for payment of German reparations (q.v.), worked out by an Allied commission headed by Charles G. Dawes. It contained the following features: (1) Evacuation of the Ruhr. (2) A new issue of money to replace the inflated marks. (3) Reparation payments should be one billion gold marks for the first year and should rise gradually to two-and-one-half billion gold marks a year. (4) A foreign loan of 800 million gold marks should be floated. (5) Reparations should be paid out of taxes imposed on railways, alcohol, tobacco, beer, sugar, and customs. (6) An Agent-General should be in charge of the execution of the plan.

D-Day Name applied to the UNITED NATIONS invasion of German-occupied France on June 6, 1944. This marked the beginning of the last stage of World War II which was to culminate in the complete military defeat of Germany within the following year.

Decartelization Program It was originally intended to break up the huge German cartels, not only because they had supported Hitler's plans for world conquest, but also because they represented a gigantic concentration of power which could not be tolerated in a truly democratic society. The Allied Military Government in 1945 set up a Decartelization Branch to wipe out German cartels. The plan had the strong support of the United States, France, and Russia. Only the British held out for a milder procedure, which would involve careful consideration of the merits of each case. In 1946, the United States came over to the British point of view, influenced by the cold war. Steps were taken to dismember I.G. Farben (the great German chemical cartel); also action was taken

50

against cartels which controlled locomotives, electrical equipment, roller-bearings, linoleum, and Diesel engines. By 1950 the decartelization program had collapsed. In the Soviet zone, huge cartels have been formed under Soviet sponsorship. The stock of giant companies producing all kinds of products is controlled by a master cartel called "Soviet Industries."

de Gasperi, Alcide Premier of Italy in post-World War II era. A Christian Democrat, he was confronted by widespread violent strikes inspired by Communists in 1947. In energetic fashion he met the challenge of one of the largest Communist parties in the world, aided by American threats to intervene if the liberty of Italy were threatened.

De Gaulle, Charles (1890-) French soldier and politician. He served with distinction in the First World War. In 1921 he served in Poland under Weygand. In 1934 he wrote *The Army of the Future*, in which he foresaw the mobile war of the future. Made brigadier general (1940), he was undersecretary of state for national defense in the Reynaud cabinet. At the time of the German-French armistice, he flew to London, where he organized the Free French Forces. He proclaimed a provisional government for France in June, 1944. He returned to Paris (Aug. 26, 1944). His government was not recognized by the Allies until Oct. 1944. He was elected provisional president of the new French republic (Nov. 1945) but resigned (Jan. 1946) when the left-wing parties ceased to support him. Always believing that he had a personal mission to "save" his country, he returned to politics in 1947, as the head of the "Reunion of the French People." This party did not prove successful and De Gaulle retired from active politics, but returned once more to an active role in 1958, when he became Premier and set out to give France a new constitution.

Democracy From two Greek words, demos meaning

"people" and kratos meaning "rule." In the United States this has come to mean the right of the people to vote and to hold public office. Although not completely provided for in the original Constitution these rights have become more firmly established by amendments to that document and by the political growth of the nation. Today members of the House of Representatives, the Senate, and the ELECTORAL COLLEGE are elected by UNIVERSAL MANHOOD SUFFRAGE.

Destroyers-for-bases deal (Sept. 2, 1940) An exchange between Great Britain and the United States, consummated through an exchange of letters between Ambassador Lord Lothian and Secretary of State Hull. The United States acquired the right to lease naval and air bases in Newfoundland, Bermuda, the Bahamas, Jamaica, St. Lucia, Trinidad, Antiqua, and British Guiana. The right to bases in Newfoundland and Bermuda were gifts. The right to the others was secured in exchange for 50 over-age destroyers. The leases were for 99 years, free of rent.

De Valera, Eamon (1882-) Irish patriot and statesman. Born in New York City of Spanish and Irish parentage, he took an active part in the Easter Rebellion of 1916. He was imprisoned several times for his activities. He led the Sinn Fein (1917-26) and then the Free State Opposition (Fianna Fail). He was president of the executive council, (1932-37) and, under the new constitution, prime minister (1937-48). During World War II he maintained strict neutrality. He became Prime Minister again in March, 1957 and still holds that office.

Dialectical Materialism A theory developed by Karl Marx. It is a deterministic philosophical system describing history with the use of Hegelian terms. Events occur in terms of thesis, antithesis and synthesis. The thesis event produces its own antithesis event which eventually destroys the thesis event producing a new synthesis. Social and religious "superstructures" are reflections of economic events. In the modern era capitalism produces the proletariat, which in turn destroys capitalism and enters the period of socialism and eventually communism. Modern socialism and communism are based in large part on the theory of dialectical materialism. The theory created a relativistic system based on the contemporary economic situation.

Disarmament The U.S. has participated in various international conferences designed to reduce the burden of armaments. The first major attempt was the WASHINGTON NAVAL CONFERENCE of 1921-22. Although the United States was never a member of the LEAGUE OF NATIONS it participated in the GENEVA CONVENTION of 1927. The United States also took part in the discussions at the LONDON CONFERENCES in 1930 and 1936. The United States was one of the major powers engaged in the disarmament discussions called by the UNITED NATIONS in Paris in December, 1951.

Displaced Persons Persons uprooted from their homes during World War II. By the Displaced Persons Act of June 25, 1948 Congress permitted the admission of 205,000 European displaced persons, including 3,000 orphans, into the United States. On June 16, 1950 the Act was amended to allow 415,744 displaced persons to enter the United States, and eliminated certain discriminatory provisions of the earlier measure. The Displaced Persons Commission reported on January 2, 1952 that it had resettled 300,000 persons in the United States, and that 36,000 more would be admitted within two months. This number is about 30 percent of all displaced persons resettled, and is the largest taken by any nation. The total cost for resettling these people was $100,601,000. In March, 1952 President TRUMAN called for emergency legislation to provide for the admission of 300,000 more displaced persons in addition to the 339,494 Europeans who had migrated to the United States by December 31, 1951. By the summer of 1952 the only congressional action on this proposal was a pending omnibus bill providing for the merger of the Immigration Acts of 1917 and 1924 and 200 additional laws, treaties, executive orders, proclamations, rules, and regulations dealing with immigration. After the unsuccessful Hungarian Revolution of October, 1956, the United States admitted to this country 21,500 Hungarian refugees.

Dollar Diplomacy A term used to describe the United States economic penetration of Central America in the first quarter of the twentieth century.

Dollar Gap A term describing the debtor relation of Western European countries to the U.S. in the post-World War II period.

Drang nach Osten (drive to east) Imperialistic phrase used to describe German ambitions (1875-1914) in northern Asia Minor if Turkey were befriended. The aim was a German corridor all the way from Bagdad to the Persian Gulf. For this, Germany supported her ally, the Dual Monarchy in southeastern Europe, while furthering the joint policy of strengthening Turkey. It was again the compelling force behind Hitler's maneuvers in June, 1941 when his hold on Western Europe seemed secure and when he pursued his dream of Eastern conquest by the massive, ill-fated invasion of Russia.

Dulles, John Foster (1888-) Statesman, b. Wash. D. C. Graduated, Princeton (1908), George Washington Univ. Law School (1911). Participant in Paris Peace Conference (1919) and U.N. organizing conference, San Francisco (1945). Drafted Japanese Peace Treaty and Pacific Treaties. U.S. Ambassador-at-large (1951). Appointed Secretary of State 1953.

Dumbarton Oaks Conference A meeting in 1944 at Dumbarton Oaks, a mansion near Washington, D. C., which laid down the foundations of the UNITED NATIONS. The attending nations included the United States, the Soviet Union, Great Britain, and China. The proposals therein adopted provided for the creation of an organization of nations for the maintenance of world peace. These proposals led to the calling of the United Nations organizational conference at San Francisco in April, 1945.

Dunkirk Treaty (1947) A mutual alliance treaty between Great Britain and France. This was to guard against any future German aggressions.

E

Eastern European Mutual Assistance Treaty (1955) Also called the Warsaw Pact. A treaty of mutual defense among the communist countries; the USSR, Poland, Albania, Czechoslovakia, Bulgaria, the German Democratic Republic, Romania and Hungary. It was set up in opposition to N.A.T.O., and the Western European Union.

Easter Rebellion (1916) An uprising in Ireland aimed at expelling the British and setting up an Irish Republic. The rebels were radicals who had left the Irish Nationalist Party to form an Irish Republican Brotherhood. Most of the "Brothers" were also members of the Sinn Fein (q.v.). Germany had promised aid by land, sea, and air, but could not help because of the British blockade. The British put down the rebellion within a week, shot a number of leaders, and placed Ireland under martial law. Several thousand were arrested and many were deported to Britain.

Ebert, Friedrich (1871-1925) First president of the Weimar Republic of Germany (elected 1919). A saddler by trade, he became a Social Democratic journalist and a member of the Reichstag (1912). He became chairman of the Social Democratic Party in 1913. He was a leader of the Revolution of 1918.

Economic and Social Council of the UN (ECOSOC) ECOSOC is composed of 18 members elected by the General Assembly for 3-year terms. Six members are replaced each year. Decisions are made by majority vote of the members present, each member having one vote. ECOSOC works through specialized committees. It recommends action to various nations, and cannot compel any nation to carry out its recommendations. Among the commissions which work for ECOSOC are the following: Commission on Human Rights (q.v.); Population Commission; Statistical Commission; Commission on Narcotic Drugs; Commission on the Status of Women; Economic and Employment Commission; Economic Commission for Latin America; Economic Commission for Asia and the Far East; Economic Commission for Europe. Certain specialized agencies are autonomous bodies. Their work is coordinated by ECOSOC (See International Labor Organization, International Bank for Reconstruction and Development, International Monetary Fund, UNESCO, World Health Organization, Food and Agricultural Organization).

Economic Warfare The conduct of an economic program designed to limit the economic capacity of an active or potential enemy. Economic warfare is undertaken through the media of export embargoes, government trading, freezing of foreign assets, exchange controls and operations, international allocation of shipping, control of critical materials, and re-export controls. During and after World War II the United States conducted an economic warfare program by means of LEND-LEASE, TRUMAN DOCTRINE, EUROPEAN RECOVERY PROGRAM, NORTH ATLANTIC TREATY, and POINT FOUR

PROGRAM. As part of this policy, the federal government undertook to control domestic buying and selling, develop special exchange procedures and financial operations, regulate its trade with neutral countries, and exercise foreign asset control.

Eden, Robert Anthony (1897-) British statesman. After service in the first World War, he entered politics (1923) as a Conservative. He devoted himself to foreign affairs, particularly to matters pertaining to the League of Nations. He resigned in 1938 because of the appeasement policy of the government. Dominion Secretary (1939), War Secretary (1940), Foreign Secretary (1940-45; 51-55). Prime Minister 1955-1956.

Edward VIII (1894-) Eldest son of George V, he served in both the navy and army during World War I. As Prince of Wales he traveled much, and was known as the "foremost salesman of the British Empire." He succeeded his father Jan. 20, 1936, but abdicated the following Dec. 11 on account of general disapprobation of his proposed marriage to a divorced American. He was given the title of Duke of Windsor and the marriage took place June 3, 1937. He was governor of the Bahamas (1940-45). Returned to private life, living most of the time in America and France.

Egyptian Military Coup d'Etat (1952) As a result of the corruption of the government, a group of young officers (the Free Officers' Movement) headed by General Naguib and Colonel NASSER, overthrew the monarchy and established a republic. All titles of nobility were proscribed and social reforms were planned. King Farouk was deposed and exiled.

Eisenhower, Dwight David (1890-) Army officer, b. Texas. Graduated, U.S.M.A., West Point (1915); member, American military mission to the PHILIPPINE ISLANDS (1935-39); brigadier general (1941); chief of war plans division, U.S.; general staff (1942); commander of allied forces in the NORTH AFRICAN

INVASION (Nov. 1942); general, supreme allied commander in western Mediterranean in charge of the INVASION OF SICILY (July 1943) and Italy; commander-in-chief of allied forces in western Europe (from Dec. 1943); in charge of the invasion of Normandy (June 1944) and western Germany; 5 star general of the army (Dec. 1944); U.S. member of Allied Control Commission for Germany; chief of staff of U.S. Army (Nov. 1945); resigned (1948); appointed president of Columbia University (1948); appointed chief of NATO (1950); elected President of the United States (1952); stricken by a coronary thrombosis in September, 1955, which delayed announcement of his candidacy for reelection in 1956 until February of that year. Reelected 1956.

Eisenhower Doctrine (1957) A unilateral declaration by PRESIDENT EISENHOWER, on March 9, 1957, to give military aid to any Near Eastern nation that requests such aid because of defense against armed aggression.

El Bekkai, Si M'Barek Ben Mustafa (1907-) Moroccan statesman. Moroccan Prime Minister, (1956-).

Elite Guards (Schutzstaffeln; SS) An organization of especially picked Nazis who were assigned to act as bodyguards for the Nazi leaders and to carry out very difficult missions. They wore a black blouse decorated with a white skull. See Schutzstaffeln.

Elizabeth II (1926-) Queen of Great Britain and head of the British Commonwealth of Nations (1952-). She succeeded her father, George VI, in February, 1952. In 1947 she married Philip Mountbatten, the Duke of Edinburgh. Her two children are H.R.H. Prince Charles, b. Buckingham Palace, November 14, 1948 and H.R.H. Princess Anne, b. Clarence House, August 15, 1950.

Enosis A Greek term meaning union with Greece. The Greek-speaking majority on the island of Cyprus is in active rebellion against the British colonial rule, fighting for a union with Greece. The movement is supposedly headed by the Archbishop Makarios.

Entente Cordiale An agreement cemented in 1904 between Britain and France by the French foreign minister Delcassé and facilitated by King Edward VII. It provided that France would recognize the priority of England in Egypt in return for a green light for France in Morocco. Secretly each gave the other a green light in the specified country should she decide to alter the existing situation.

EOKA Underground Cypriot organization which has generally rallied to the leadership of Archbishop Makarios but in recent months shows signs of ignoring the exiled churchman and following their military Chief, Colonel Grivas, who is uncompromising on the matter of independence for Cyprus.

Euratom The European Atomic Energy Community, composed of six nations: West Germany, France, Italy, the Netherlands, Belgium, and Luxemburg, banded together for the purpose of promoting the development of atomic power in Western Europe.

European Coal and Steel Community (1952) An inter-European body that controls the pricing, production and marketing of coal and steel in Italy, France, the German Federal Republic, and the Benelux nations.

European Defense Community A six nation army established by a TREATY signed on May 27, 1952 by the GERMAN FEDERAL REPUBLIC, France, Italy, Belgium, the Netherlands and Luxemburg. It provided for establishment of a European Army; the treaty contained 131 clauses and 9 protocols in which the member nations pledged a peace-time army for 50 years wearing a single style uniform, receiving the same pay, and commanded by a mixed general staff. It also set up a ruling council, an advisory chamber, a court of ARBITRATION, and an operative commission. France was pledged to contribute 14 divisions, Germany and

Italy 12 divisions each, and the other three powers a joint total of 5 divisions. Accompanying the treaty was a declaration by the United States and Great Britain to defend the six nations and the Allied-held sectors of Berlin against attack "from any quarter" and to guarantee the integrity and unity of the new army. The pledge was designed specifically to assure France against a German withdrawal. Three of the protocols set out the close relationship of the European Army with the NORTH ATLANTIC TREATY Organization and included a mutual aid pact with England and a formula for financing the army. The link with NATO established the first alliance in history to include the United States, Britain, France, and Germany. The treaty was subject to the ratifications of the member nations and has never been put into effect because of France's failure to ratify it.

European Payments Union This scheme, suggested by ECA Administrator (MARSHALL PLAN, q.v.), Paul G. Hoffman, was adopted July 1, 1950. Seventeen European nations and the sterling bloc have subscribed to it. The initial working capital came from ECA grants and contributions from the participating countries. The funds are deposited in the BANK OF INTERNATIONAL SETTLEMENT (Basel) (q.v.) and are managed by a committee of seven appointed by the OEEC. The purpose of the Union is to provide credit for purchases of foreign goods.

Export Import Bank A government corporation chartered by Congress in 1934. It was established by EXECUTIVE ORDER in that year but was provided a statutory basis and additional powers by Congress in 1945. Its functions are to make loans directly or guarantee private loans in periods when private credit resources are scarce. The purpose of such loans is to finance COMMERCE between the United States and its possessions as well as with foreign nations. Its authorized capital is $1,000,000,000. Whether in the form of guarantees or loans its obligations may equal three and one half times its capitalization. In the fiscal year 1951 its expenditures were $87,692,961.08. In that period its foreign loans reached $352,000,000.

Extradition, international The exchange of escaped prisoners or persons on bail from one nation to another. These exchanges are accomplished by treaties between the nations. As is typical under international law the governments of these nations interpret the treaties, thus frequently refusing demand for extradition. An outstanding recent illustration of extradition TREATY interpretation was the refusal of Great Britain to return Gerhart Eisler, who had jumped bail in 1949 and fled the jurisdiction of the United States.

Extraterritoriality Special rights conferred by a government upon the CITIZENS and subjects of other nations who are resident within the conferring nation. Such rights have in the past included exemption from laws of the conferring nation and/or privileges pertaining to railroad concessions, harbor rights, and TAXATION.

F

Faisal II (1935-1958) King of Iraq under regent (1939-1953). Assumed active leadership in 1953. Proclaimed King of the ARAB FEDERAL STATE OF JORDAN and IRAQ in February 1958. The king was killed in the recent Iraq Revolution (July, 1958) which dissolved this union with Jordan and set up a republic in Iraq.

Falange Española Tradicionalista y de las Juntas de Ofensiva Nacional Sindicalistas The Spanish Fascist party. The only legal party in Spain since 1939.

Fascism The movement and principles which underlay the Fascist state in Italy. Fascism stands for an inter-

61

national ideology and policy following the "doctrines" and practices of Mussolini's Italy, in this respect closely related to German National Socialism. The word is derived from the word fasces (a bundle of rods and an ax tied together), the badge of authority of the magistrates in ancient Rome. Fascism, in adopting this symbol, indicated its intention of restoring the glory of the Roman Empire. The movement had its beginnings in the interventionist group under the leadership of the former Socialist, Benito Mussolini, soon after the outbreak of World War I. It was officially created in March, 1919, as the *fasci di combattimento*. In an atmosphere of a disappointing peace settlement, economic depression and social unrest Fascism's promise of quick action appealed to dissatisfied army officers, an impoverished middle class, and industrialists afraid of Bolshevism. The movement seized power in the so-called "March on Rome" in 1922 and after an initial use of parliamentary machinery and established institutions (monarchy, army), it created a dictatorial one-party regime. Though not backed up by an elaborate and comprehensive theory of society, Fascism may be regarded as a reaction against the ideas of the French Revolution, against rationalism, liberalism, individualism. It has been influenced somewhat by modern syndicalism, and to a much greater extent by nationalistic ideas which found a fertile ground in this country of belated national unification. While Fascism's claims at being a social revolution have hardly materialized, its political dynamics have been evident in its militant structure and its international adventurers. It made good use of the slogan of a presumed "red peril" in post-war Italy. In differentiation from NATIONAL SOCIALISM, it may be regarded as a more conservative and less totalitarian system and one of primarily personal rule. Fascism is Mussolini-ism to a larger degree than National Socialism is Hitler-ism.

Federation of Malaya, Creation of the The Malayan Federation was created out of the British colonies of the Malay peninsula, Penang and Malacca, receiving independence in 1957. It became a member of the United Nations, Sept. 1957.

Fianna Fail A Republican party organized in Ireland by De Valera in opposition to the treaty of 1921 which created the Irish Free State and accepted a compromise position regarding North Ireland.

Fifth French Republic The Fifth French Republic officially came into being on October 5, 1958, when General Charles de Gaulle promulgated the new constitution which the French people recently approved in a plebiscite. Following the promulgation of the new constitution the interim French Cabinet adopted a new electoral system for the elections to the new National Assembly which are scheduled for November. The new constitution confers more powers on the president of the Republic and is designed to provide more permanence and stability to the French governments.

Five Power Treaty A treaty negotiated by the United States, Great Britain, Japan, France, and Italy at the WASHINGTON NAVAL CONFERENCE. By its terms the powers agreed to the scrapping of a number of battleships which were either afloat or in the process of construction. In the building of capital ships they agreed to a "naval holiday" until 1931 and established the following ratio for capital ship tonnage: 5:5:3 for the United States, Great Britain, and Japan, and 1.75 each for France and Italy. It limited fortifications in the PACIFIC OCEAN generally to those maintained by the signatory powers at the time. Also known as Washington Naval Treaty. See Washington Naval Conference, Four Power Treaty, and Nine Power Pact.

Five Year Plans Gigantic blueprints to increase Soviet productive capacity. Factories were to be located with reference to natural resources. The Urals and western Siberia were to be exploited. Arms production was to be stepped up drastically. The first Plan (Oct. 31, 1928-Dec. 31, 1932) nearly doubled Soviet heavy industry. The aim of the second Plan was to improve the quality and quantity of consumers' goods. A fourth Plan was begun in 1946 and completed in 1951. Its purpose was to repair wartime damage and consolidate the new West Siberia industry. A fifth Plan was announced early in 1953.

Foch, Ferdinand (1851-1929) Soldier in French Army. Served in Franco-Prussian War. When the Germans began their last great offensive he was selected to coordinate the Allied Armies on the Western front. Under this unity of command, General Foch had approximately 10,000,000 men under him and he directed five major battles which hurled back the enemy's spring offensive and eventually compelled their surrender. He was made Marshal of France in 1918.

Food and Agricultural Organization (FAO) The FAO of the UN came into existence in 1943 to plan for postwar food production. It can only advise the various nations of the world. It encourages agricultural research, supplies information about proper nutrition, seeks to stimulate more production of food, furnishes technical advice on farming methods, and promotes the more efficient distribution of food from surplus to deficit areas.

Ford, Henry (1863-1947) Industrialist. b. Dearborn, Michigan. Worked as machine shop apprentice in Detroit. Built his first automobile in 1892. Organized Ford Motor Co. (1903) Manufactured first Model T in 1909. Factory assembly methods made him world-famous. In 1915 he chartered the Ford Peace Ship which transported a group of pacifists to Europe in an effort to halt World War I by mediation. Unsuccessful candidate for U.S. Senate in 1918. President of Ford Motor Company to 1919, and again from 1943 until his death in 1947.

Foreign Policy, U.S. The United States was a major factor in world politics at the opening of World War I. It emerged out of the war as a creditor nation and, although one of the three or four great powers, retreated once more into a policy of ISOLATIONISM. This policy was negated by the nation's frequent participation in international conferences on DISARMAMENT, peace, and TRADE. The "GOOD-NEIGHBOR" POLICY of the NEW DEAL administrations restored sounder relations between Latin America and the United States. The nation's interests in the Far East and the continued aggressions of the AXIS POWERS once more turned this country to a policy of collective action to resist aggression. Unlike its refusal to join the LEAGUE OF NATIONS after World War I, the United States participated actively in the organization of the UNITED NATIONS after World War II. In the postwar world it assumed the leadership in international reconstruction and rehabilitation. Through the media of the TRUMAN DOCTRINE, MARSHALL PLAN, NORTH ATLANTIC TREATY, and MUTUAL SECURITY Program the United States showed clearly that it had turned its back to isolationism.

Formosa An island province of China located in the western Pacific ninety miles off the China coast. Its POPULATION of 7,500,000 occupies an area of 13,836 square miles. Its principal agricultural products are sugar cane, rice, bananas, pineapples, and tea. Other industries include CANNING, chemicals, wood pulp, and sugar refining. Ceded to Japan in 1895, Formosa was restored to China in 1945 in conformance with the Cairo Declaration. Although the regime of Chiang Kai-Shek was overthrown on the Chinese mainland in 1949, Formosa remained in his hands. At the outbreak of the Korean War in June, 1950 President TRUMAN ordered the United States Seventh Fleet to defend the island against any attempted invasion by the Chinese Communists. The latter government has consistently refused to renounce its sovereign rights over Formosa, this issue remaining a fundamental cause of the exclusion from the UNITED NATIONS of that government, and of the deterioration of relations between it and the United States.

Formosa Resolution (1955) An American Congressional resolution granting the President power to defend Formosa and the Pescadores, and thus to preserve the Nationalist Chinese government.

Four Freedoms, the An address by President F. D. ROOSE-VELT to Congress on January 6, 1941, outlined as the objective of World War II the survival of the Four Freedoms. These freedoms are freedom of speech and expression, freedom of worship everywhere in the world, freedom from want by securing to every nation a healthy, peaceful life for its inhabitants, and freedom from fear by the world wide reduction of armaments.

Four Power Treaty One of seven treaties emerging from the WASHINGTON NAVAL CONFERENCE in 1921. The TREATY abolished the Anglo-Japanese Alliance of 1911. It further provided that the signatory nations respect each other's possessions in the PACIFIC OCEAN, that they confer for the adjustment of controversies arising in the Far West, and that they agree on joint measures in the event of aggression in the Pacific by a non-signatory power. It recognized the legality of the mandated territories in the Pacific and, by a supplementary treaty in 1922, included among these the Pescadores, FORMOSA, and southern Sakhalin.

Fourteen Points, the (Jan. 8, 1918) In an address to Congress, President Wilson outlined the Allied war aims.

This speech paralleled an address by Lloyd George to the Trade Union Congress (Jan. 5, 1918). The Fourteen Points are as follows: (1) Open covenants of peace, openly arrived at and the abolition of secret diplomacy. (2) Freedom of the seas. (3) Removal, as far as possible, of all economic barriers. (4) Adequate guarantees, so that national armaments will be reduced to the lowest point consistent with safety. (5) Impartial adjustment of colonial claims with proper consideration of the interests of the populations concerned. (6) Evacuation of Russian territory and the free determination of its own political and national policy. (7) Evacuation and restoration of Belgium. (8) Evacuation and restoration of France and the return of Alsace-Lorraine. (9) Readjustment of the frontiers of Italy along clearly recognizable lines of nationality. (10) The freest opportunity of autonomous development for the peoples of Austria-Hungary. (11) Evacuation and restoration of Romania, Serbia, and Montenegro and free access to the sea for Serbia. (12) Autonomous development for non-Turkish possessions of the sultan and internationalization of the Dardanelles. (13) An independent Poland with access to the sea. (14) An association of nations to afford mutual guarantees of political independence and territorial integrity to great and small states alike.

Fourth Republic, Establishment of the (1946) The successor to the VICHY GOVERNMENT after the end of World War II. It reestablished parliamentary democracy in France.

Four-Year Plan, Nazi At the National Socialist Party Congress, held in Sept. 1936 in Nuremberg, Hitler announced that within four years Germany must be independent of foreign countries with respect to all those materials which could in any way be produced through "German capability, through German chem-

istry, or by our machine and mining industries." The
execution of the plan was entrusted to Göring. When
Göring and Schacht differed as to methods, the latter
resigned and was replaced as minister of economics
and head of the Reichsbank by Dr. Walther Funk.
When Austria entered the Reich (1938), the Four-
Year Plan was speedily introduced there. Chief emphasis was on development of synthetic fuel, rubber,
and fabrics; and better use of old mines.

France, Liberation of The last major campaign on the
western front in World War II began after the successful INVASION OF NORMANDY in June, 1944. On
July 9th Allied forces entered Brittany, after taking
St. Lô, and pursued the fleeing Germans toward Paris.
On August 15th an amphibious operation landed
troops on the French Mediterranean coast between
Marseilles and Nice. Supported by the uprising of
the French Forces of the Interior the Allies captured
Paris on August 25th. On September 2nd Brussels
was taken and by early December the Germans had
been driven almost completely from France and Belgium. The Allied lines stretched along the German
frontier from Holland to Switzerland. The last German counter-offensive took place in Belgium and
Luxemburg in Mid-December in the famous BATTLE
OF THE BULGE. By January, 1945 the Germans had
been repulsed and the Allies were prepared to invade
Germany.

Franco, Francisco (1892-) Dictator of Spain. Born at El
Ferrol, he entered the army and rapidly rose to the
position of general. He commanded the Spanish Foreign Legion in Morocco. In 1935 he became chief of
staff. Because he was considered to be "politically
dangerous," he was sent (1936) to govern the Canary
Islands. He flew to Morocco and started the revolution there (July, 1936). When General Sanjurjo, the
designated head of the rebellion, was killed in an

airplane crash, Franco assumed leadership of the rebellion (1936-39). With the aid of Nazi and Italian troops he overthrew the socialist government and made himself head (Caudillo) of an authoritarian state.

Free Enterprise The economic system which is characterized by the private ownership of the means of production and the investment of capital for profit purposes. As developed by the English economists Adam Smith and David Ricardo, free enterprise postulated an absence of government interference with business. In the United States its proponents have opposed government regulation of private business, and have advocated competition and the dependence upon "natural economic laws." See laissez-faire.

Free Port A port in the United States in which foreign vessels may unload cargoes for inspection, grading, and repackaging prior to trans-shipment to their ultimate destinations, without paying customs duties. In 1952 the only free port in the United States was located in Staten Island, New York.

French Alliances, the Soon after World War I France established a series of defensive alliances with Belgium (1920), Poland (1922), Czechoslovakia (1924), Romania (1926), Yugoslavia (1927), and Russia (1933), against the possibility of a German-Austrian resurgence of aggressive expansion.

French Committee of National Liberation Formed June 4, 1943 for the purpose of liberating France from the Nazis. It included both General de Gaulle and General Giraud.

French Guinea A newly formed state in West Africa, separated from the French Republic by plebiscite (September, 1958) organized at the behest of General De Gaulle. First Premier: Sekou Touré.

G

Gallipoli Campaign (April 25-Dec. 20, 1915) An attempt
to capture Constantinople by way of the Gallipoli
Peninsula. The attacking forces consisted of British,
French, and Anzac (Australian and New Zealand
Army Corps) troops. After months of futile fighting,
in which the Allied armies suffered heavily from heat
and disease, the campaign was abandoned. During
the campaign the British warships *Goliath, Triumph,*
and *Majestic* were sunk by one German submarine.
This campaign was sponsored by Sir WINSTON CHURCH-
ILL (q.v.), who at that time was First Lord of the
Admiralty. After the Gallipoli fiasco, Churchill was
forced to resign.

Gandhi, Mohandas Karamchand (1869-1948) Indian leader. He studied Law in London, then practiced Law
in India and South Africa. He began the non-coopera-
tive movement against British colonial rule in India
(1919). He became the leader of the Indian National
Congress (1925). He was imprisoned innumerable
times because of his policy of civil disobedience. He
was opposed to force and violence for revolutionary
means. Advocating complete independence he opposed
the Government of India Acts (1919 & 1935) as too
limited. Gandhi had also been influential in breaking
down the caste system in India. He was assassinated
in Jan. 1948, just after the end of British rule.

General Agreement on Tariffs and Trade (1947) A series
of tariff agreements negotiated through the International Trade Organization. An international agreement,
it decidedly lowered trade barriers between many
nations.

General Assembly of the UN This body is the principal
organ of discussion in the UN. All member nations
are represented, and each delegation (five or less) has
one vote. Important questions require a two-third

70

majority; other questions are decided by a simple majority. The General Assembly meets once a year, although it may be called into special session. The General Assembly does not make laws. It only *recommends* actions to the member nations, the Security Council, or other UN agencies. It admits new members, suspends or expels present members, elects the Secretary-General, elects the non-permanent members of the other agencies, draws up the budget, creates new agencies, and elects judges of the World Court.

General Strike, the British (May 3-12, 1926) This strike was called in sympathy with the coal miners. It involved about 2½ million of the 6 million trade-union members in Britain. Volunteers maintained essential services. The Trade Union Council called off the strike May 12 on the promise that wage negotiations would be resumed. However, the coal miners continued to strike until Nov. 19, when they gave up unconditionally. The original difficulty began with the curtailment in use of coal and consequent retrenchment in employment and wage cuts.

Geneva Naval Conference A conference which met at Geneva, Switzerland from June 20, to August 24, 1927. It was called at the proposal of President Coolidge to discuss the extension to smaller types of vessels of the naval DISARMAMENT treaties of the WASHINGTON NAVAL CONFERENCE. Japan and Great Britain attended the Conference. France and Italy declined the invitation. The United States delegation proposed to extend the 5:5:3 ratio to other types of vessels and to limit the tonnage in each class as well as the size of guns and torpedo tubes. England attempted to retain freedom in the construction of 7,500 ton cruisers. The United States opposed England's demand, requesting in turn a small number of 10,000 ton cruisers. The failure to reconcile the Anglo-American proposals brought the Conference to an unsuccessful conclusion.

71

Geneva Protocol, the (Oct. 2, 1924) This was the product of efforts to strengthen international machinery and to overcome the weakness in the League, due to the absence of the United States, Germany, and the Soviet Union. It was a treaty of mutual assistance in which an aggressor was defined and schemes were proposed to contain and punish all acts of aggression. It provided for compulsory arbitration of all disputes and outlined a course of action for all signatory nations in case of warfare. Although many small nations were enthusiastic for the Protocol the agreement was never adopted. The greatest opposition came from the British dominions.

Geneva Summit Conference (1955) The Big Four (President Eisenhower, Prime Minister Anthony Eden, Premier Edgar Faure, and Premier Bulganin) met in Geneva for six days beginning July 18, 1955. Russia opposed unification of Germany. President Eisenhower advanced a new proposal on disarmament which provided exchange with Russia of military blue prints showing location and strength of each country's armed forces; and allowed aerial reconnaissance of each other's military installations. The West urged the lifting of the Iron Curtain and the interchange of personal travel, ideas, and information between East and West. To explore further the topics discussed at the Summit Conference, a subsequent meeting of the Foreign Ministers was arranged to take place on Oct. 27, 1955, in Geneva. The Eisenhower proposals on armaments were turned over to a 5 power subcommittee of the U. N. Disarmament Commission. Nothing of consequence developed after proposals were referred to subsequent meeting of the Foreign Ministers.

George II (1890-1947) Grecian monarch. Succeeded in 1922 when his father Constantine I was deposed for the second time. George was deposed in 1923, but was restored in 1935. He was in exile in England during the German occupation of his country (1941-1944). He returned to Greece in 1946 after a plebiscite approved his return.

George V (1865-1936) King of Great Britain and Northern Ireland: Emperor of India (1910-36). Second son of Edward VII. He became heir apparent (1892) when his brother, the duke of Clarence, died. Chief events of his reign were World War I (1914-18), the agreement with the Irish Free State (1921), the Great Depression of the 1930's and the Commonwealth (Westminster) Conference.

George VI (1895-1952) King of Great Britain and Emperor of the British Empire (1936-52). Second son of George V he became king when his elder brother abdicated in Dec. 1936. Because of great devotion to duty during the Second World War and post-war years, his health was undermined.

German Democratic Republic (East Germany) This region, which is under Soviet control, is the home of about 18 million people. It contains some of the best farm land of prewar Germany, as well as Berlin, the historic capital of the country. The government of East Germany was set up by the Soviets in October, 1949, to rival the newly-created Bonn Republic.

German Federal Republic (West Germany) This region, which was originally occupied by Britain, France, and the United States, after the Second World War, contains 75% of the normal population of Germany, 70% of the minerals, 80% of the coal, and 85% of the steel industry. It contains also the seaports on the North Sea. However, it contains relatively little agriculture. By the Occupation Statute of 1948, terms were set by which a constitution could be prepared for this region. By this statute, it was decided that West Germany should have a federal republic, composed of

Länder (states). The Allied Military Government was to be replaced by three civilian High Commissioners from the United States, Great Britain, and France, who should have veto powers in the fields of reparations and security. German representatives met at Bonn in Sept. 1948, and prepared a constitution. The German Federal Republic was established on September 21, 1949 when the Allied Control Council turned over to it the administration of the United States, British, and French zones of occupation. This step marked the culmination of a series of political and economic moves designed to restore German sovereignty and modify the restrictions on German industry laid down in the Yalta and Potsdam Declarations. In January, 1947 the United States and England agreed to treat their zones as a single area for economic purposes. In February, 1948 these nations created an economic council to regulate economic affairs in their zones. In April, 1949 the three western powers adopted the Occupation Statute establishing the basis for a merger of the United States, British, and French Zones. The Bonn Constitution for Western Germany became effective on May 23, 1949. Parliamentary elections were held on August 14, a President elected on September 12, and on September 15, the lower house confirmed the appointment of Konrad Adenauer as Chancellor. Bonn was selected as the federal capital on November 3. On May 5, 1955, France and Great Britain announced ratification of the Paris Agreements which ended the 10 year occupation and established West Germany as a sovereign state. On May 9, 1955 the republic became a full member of NATO.

German Peace Contract A series of 15 "contractual agreements" signed on May 26, 1952 by the United States, Great Britain, France and the GERMAN FEDERAL REPUBLIC. The agreements technically ended the OCCU-

PATION OF GERMANY by the three Allied Powers, but provided for the stay in West Germany of the 500,000 Allied troops there at the time of signing. Other provisions included a financial agreement whereby West Germany was to split her defense BUDGET between the maintenance of Allied forces and 12 German divisions for the new European Army, an arbitration agreement to cover future disputes, a protocol pledging the Allies to remain in the western sector of Berlin, and a troop agreement pertaining to the relations between West Germany and the Allied troops. The Western Powers retained the right to maintain defense forces as long as the international situation makes it necessary, to intervene to restore order in West Germany in the event of attack from the outside, and to negotiate with the Soviet Union over Berlin and German unification. Allied forces were thereafter to be subject to German law and to continue the use of special "occupational currency." Other provisions included clauses dealing with the settlement of matters arising out of the war and the occupation, decartelization, the continuance of property restitution to Nazi victims, and compensation for injuries suffered in concentration camps. The contract repealed the occupation statute, abolished the ALLIED HIGH COMMISSION, and placed relations between the German Federal Republic and the Allied Powers on a government-to-government basis with the exchange of ambassadors. The document was subject to the ratification of the signatory powers.

Germany, Battle of After the defeat of the Germans at the BATTLE OF THE BULGE the Western Allies coordinated their defenses with the Russians moving in from Poland. At the end of January, 1945 a combined Anglo-American-Canadian Army, of which two-thirds were Americans, massed for the final campaign. The British Twenty-First Army Group was commanded by Field Marshal Montgomery in the north. In the center the American Twelfth Army Group was commanded by General Bradley. In the south General Devers commanded the American Sixth Army Group which included French troops. On February 7th the United States Third Army crossed the German frontier in 10 places. The next day British and Canadian troops moved forward from Holland. By March 5th American troops had crossed the Saar River and advanced into the Ruhr, having captured a total of 954,377 prisoners since D-Day. With the breach in the German "West Wall" defense, Trier and Cologne fell in March. On March 8th the Rhine River was crossed and by the end of the month all the Allied armies were beyond the Rhine. On April 18th the Third Army under General Patton reached Czechoslovakia. On April 11th the United States Ninth Army reached the Elbe River. By April 29th German resistance in northern Italy was broken and German troops surrendered unconditionally on May 2nd. On that day Russian troops entered Berlin from the East, and on May 7th Admiral Doenitz, who had been proclaimed head of the German government after Hitler's alleged suicide on April 29th, surrendered unconditionally. On May 8th President Truman and Prime Minister Churchill proclaimed V-E Day, the end of the war in Europe.

Gestapo   In 1933 Hitler instituted the German secret police (Geheime Staatspolizei), Gestapo, which, was to root out any anti-Nazi individuals or organizations in Germany and subsequently conquered countries. The name became a synonym for secret police that used brutality and terrorism in their operations.

Ghana, Creation of (1957)   On March 6, 1957 the Republic of Ghana was created out of the Gold Coast colony of Great Britain. It subsequently joined the

British Commonwealth. KWAME NKRUMAH is the Prime Minister (1957-).

Gilbert Islands, Battle of the Several of the Gilbert Islands were taken by Japan at the opening of World War II. In November, 1943 the Marines, supported by off-shore naval and air bombardment, recaptured them in one of the bloodiest battles of the Pacific war.

Giraud, Henri Honoré (1879-1949) French general. He served with distinction during World War I and the Riff campaign (1925-26). Captured by the Germans in World War II, he made a dramatic escape (April, 1942). It was the Anglo-American wish that he should command the French forces in exile.

Goebbels, Paul Joseph (1897-1945) Nazi politician. A brilliant student of history, philosophy, and psychology, he took a leading part in organizing the Nazi Party. He became Hitler's famous propaganda chief (1929) and minister (1933). In the last days of Nazidom, he committed suicide, along with his wife and seven children.

"Good Neighbor Policy" The popular phrase applied to the Latin American policy of the early administrations of F. D. Roosevelt. It signified the reversal of the earlier "Big Stick'" and "DOLLAR DIPLOMACY" foreign policies of the Theodore Roosevelt and Taft administrations. The good neighbor policy was manifested by the withdrawal of the remaining American marines from Haiti, Santo Domingo, Cuba, and Nicaragua, the amicable settlement of the railroad and land disputes with Mexico in 1936 and 1938, and the abrogation of the Platt Amendment. The statement of this policy was declared at the Seventh Pan American Conference at MONTEVIDEO in 1933. Since then, relations between the United States and Latin-America have been sound.

Göring, Hermann Wilhelm (1893-1946) German aviator

and statesman. Born in Rosenheim in Bavaria, he became a famous aviator during World War I. Upon the death of Richthofen, Göring became commander of the former's "Flying Circus." He became a Nazi and took part in the "BEER-HALL PUTSCH" in 1923 (q.v.). When Hitler came into power (1933), Göring became one of his chief collaborators. He was creator and marshal of the Luftwaffe, and from 1936 was economic dictator of Germany. In 1939 he was named Hitler's successor. In the last days of the regime he disappeared, but was captured by the Americans. Condemned to death at the NUREMBERG TRIALS (q.v.), he escaped execution by suicide.

Gosplan (1921)   USSR state planning commission.

Government of Ireland Act (Dec. 23, 1920)   A law passed by the British Parliament which provided for home rule for Ireland, but which separated Ireland into two parts, Northern & Southern Ireland.

Government Ownership   The system in which the state owns and operates business enterprises. In the United States the federal, state, and municipal governments own many enterprises, particularly in the field of Public Utilities. Federally chartered corporations operate railroads, hotels, restaurants, barge lines, hydroelectric plants, armories, shipyards, merchant shipping lines, and banking facilities. Among the prominent corporations are the Panama Canal Company, the Inland Waterways Corporation, the Tennessee Valley Authority, and the Reconstruction Finance Corporation.

Great Depression   The extreme economic crisis which, with minor upswings, beset the United States from 1929 to 1940. It began with the stock market crash of 1929 and led to an economic decline that witnessed no recovery until the spring of 1933. In every field of business endeavor huge losses were suffered, with

the consequent rise of unemployment and social upheavals. Exports declined from $5,241,000,000 in
1929 to $1,611,000,000 in 1933. In that period im-
ports fell from $4,399,000,000 to $1,323,000,000.
Unemployment rose from 3,000,000 to an estimated
17,000,000. Wholesale prices declined from an average index of 95.3 to 65.9. Commercial failures increased from 24,000 in 1928 to 32,000 in 1932, and
more than 5,000 banks failed in the first three years
of the Great Depression. Factory payrolls fell below
half the 1929 level, and total paid wages declined
from $55,000,000,000 to $33,000,000,000 in 1931.
Except for public construction, building virtually
ceased, and the national income declined from $85,-
000,000,000 on the eve of the Depression to $37,-
000,000,000 in 1932. Similar hardships befell the
farmer, aggravating economic dislocations which had
been his lot since the end of World War I. Despite
minor and temporary upswings, full recovery was not
achieved until the defense and war programs after
1940.

Grey, Sir Edward, Viscount Grey of Fallodon (1862-1933)
British statesman. Born in Northumberland. Educated
at Oxford. For many years a prominent figure in the
British Foreign Office. As secretary of state for foreign
affairs (1905-16) he negotiated the Triple Entente,
took an active part in Balkan affairs, and steered the
course of Britain in the early days of World War I.
He resigned (1916) because of poor health and failing
eyesight. Chancellor of Oxford (1928). Author of
Twenty-five Years, 1892-1916 (1925).

Grotewohl, Otto (1894-) German communist and statesman. Prime minister of the German Democratic Republic (1949-).

Guadalcanal, Battle of The first military offensive of the
United States in World War II. Following the defeat

of the Japanese fleet at the Battles of the CORAL SEA
and MIDWAY the United States came to the decision
to assume the offensive in the Pacific. On August 7,
1942 the battle began with a combined air and sea
attack on Guadalcanal in the SOLOMON ISLANDS. Marines landed and established a beachhead on Guadalcanal and the island of Tulagi, capturing them after
months of severe fighting. Under Admiral WILLIAM
F. HALSEY JR. the American fleet soundly defeated the
Japanese in the naval battle off Guadalcanal between
November 13 and 15 in what has been referred to
as the greatest naval battle since Jutland. By February, 1943 the last Japanese troops had been driven
off the island, and the first success in the stepping
stone strategy to the Japanese mainland had been
achieved.

Guam The largest of the Mariana Islands in the Pacific
Ocean. It is 206 square miles in area and had a population in 1950 of 59,498. Its chief products are copra,
coconut oil, bananas, pineapples, and corn. Guam
came into the possession of the United States as a
result of the Treaty of Paris of 1898 after the Spanish-
American War. From then until August 1, 1950 it was
administered by the Department of the Navy. On
December 11, 1941 the island was captured by Japan.
It was retaken on July 27, 1944. Prior to 1950 Guamanians were considered nationals of the United States,
their political and civil rights subject to the control
of the naval officer in command of the island. In that
year the Organic Act of Guam transferred administration to the Department of the Interior and established a Unicameral Legislature elected biennially by
the permanent residents. Guamanians were made
citizens of the United States.

Guinea: During the campaign for ratification of the new
constitution General Charles de Gaulle warned that
any French possession that rejected the constitution

would be cut off from France and regarded as independent. Ignoring this warning, the French West African territory of Guinea voted overwhelmingly to reject the constitution. Immediately General de Gaulle cut Guinea off from French authority and announced that the area would no longer receive administrative or financial aid from France. Already, however, Guinea has made overtures to France for an association with France for cooperative development under Article 88 of the new constitution.

H

Hague Conferences Two international conferences at The Hague in Holland called for the purpose of dealing with the problems of WAR, DISARMAMENT, and international disputes. The first conference met in 1899 and was attended by an American delegation headed by Andrew D. White, American Ambassador to Germany. The conference adopted rules for the mitigation of the cruelties of war, and established the PERMANENT COURT OF ARBITRATION. The U. S. A. was the first great nation to submit a case for ARBITRATION to this tribunal (1902). The second conference was called in 1907 with delegates from 44 nations meeting in the Peace Palace built by ANDREW CARNEGIE. The conference adopted the DRAGO DOCTRINE, which advocated a limitation on the use of force in recovering contract debts, and a series of resolutions looking toward the more humane conduct of war, the protection of the rights of neutrals, the use of the SUBMARINE, and the bombing of ports. The attempts of the American delegation under the leadership of JOSEPH H. CHOATE to persuade the Conference to adopt a plan for the limitation of naval armaments and to create a permanent international court of justice failed.

81

Haile Selassie I (1891-) Emperor of Ethiopia (1930-) He was ousted from Ethiopia (1936) by the Italian invaders. He recaptured Ethiopia (1941) leading the Ethiopian army from the Anglo-Egyptian Sudan.

Haiti A Republic in the Caribbean Sea. Its 1952 population of 3,150,000 occupies an area of 10,748 square miles, comprising the western third of the island of Hispaniola. Since 1843, the eastern two-thirds have constituted the DOMINICAN REPUBLIC. The island is thus the only one in the world containing two sovereign nations. Haiti established its independence in 1804, following its revolt against France three years earlier. The United States intervened in 1915 to protect American economic interests in the National Bank and National Railroad and to forestall European intervention during the revolution which had broken out in 1911. Americans thereafter served as officials of the Haitian government, exercising control over its public works, sanitation, finances, and police activities. In 1922 the President of the United States appointed John H. Russell as American high commissioner in Haiti to supervise improvements in highways, irrigation, and sanitation. A loan of $16,000,000 granted by American banks in that year contributed to the financing of these ventures. By TREATIES of 1916 and 1924 with Haiti, American MARINES remained until 1934 at which time they were removed in conformance with the "GOOD NEIGHBOR" policy of the first F. D. ROOSEVELT administration. The occupation of Haiti was part of the program known as "DOLLAR DIPLOMACY", and was attacked by Latin-America as "YANKEE IMPERIALISM."

Halifax, Edward Frederick Lindley Wood, First Earl of (1881-) British statesman. He entered Parliament as a Conservative (1910). President of the Board of Education (1924) and Minister of Agriculture and Fisheries (1924-25). Viceroy of India (as Baron Irwin)

(1926-31). Foreign Secretary (1938-40). Ambassador to the United States (1941-46).

Halsey, William Frederick (1882-) Admiral. b. New Jersey. Graduated, U.S.N.A., Annapolis (1904); commander of destroyer squadrons in World War I; interested in naval aviation; assigned to carrier units (after 1935); during World War II responsible for raids on the MARSHALL AND GILBERT ISLANDS (January, 1942) and commanded attack on the Solomon Islands (August, 1942); appointed commander of the South Pacific theatre; commander of United States 3rd fleet (1944-45); led action against the PHILIPPINES (1945) and Japan (1945); became admiral of the fleet (November, 1945); retired because of ill health (1947).

Hammarskjold, Dag Hjalmar Agne Carl (1905-) United Nations leader. He became Secretary-General of the UNITED NATIONS (1953) after leaving the position of Deputy Foreign Affairs Minister of Sweden.

Harding, Warren Gamaliel (1865-1923) Twenty-ninth President of the United States. b. Ohio. Owner and editor of Marion *Star* in Ohio (from 1884); served in state senate and was lieutenant governor of state; elected U.S. Senator (1915-21); prominent Republican who favored PROTECTIVE TARIFF and opposed the League of Nations; elected President (1921-23); although he had many able men in his administration he also appointed corrupt officials; died while on speaking tour at San Francisco (Aug. 2, 1923) before exposure of his Secretary of the Interior Fall and Attorney-General Daugherty on charges of corruption and fraud.

Havana Conference A Pan American Conference held at Havana, Cuba in July 1940. It proposed a treaty setting up an Inter-American Commission of Territorial Administration to assume control of and supervise all Latin-American territories concerning which there might be a "transfer or intent to transfer sovereignty."

Although never established the mere proposal to set up such an agency was sufficient to forestall any attempted Axis invasion of the western hemisphere. The term, Havana Conference, is also used to refer to the Sixth International Conference of American States meeting from Jan. 16 to Feb. 20, 1928. At this Conference progress was made in providing for conciliation in Latin-American disputes and for international cooperation in cultural matters.

Hawley-Smoot Tariff Act   One of the highest TARIFFS in American history. It was enacted in 1930 and raised the high duties of the Fordney-McCumber Tariff. The average of all schedules was increased. One-third of the items were changed, 890 being raised, including 50 transfers from the free to the tax list. Two hundred and thirty-five items were reduced, including 75 transfers from the dutiable to the free list. Cement, boots, shoes, and hides were made dutiable. The average rate upon agricultural raw materials was increased from 38.10 to 48.92 percent, while other commodities were increased from 31.02 to 34.30 percent. Heavy increases were made on minerals, chemicals, dyestuffs, and textiles. It was estimated that the average for all dutiable articles was 41.57 percent as compared to the Fordney-McCumber average of 38.24. The act hastened the decline in world trade and aroused deep resentment abroad. In the United States farmers and manufacturers with export surpluses and bankers with foreign investments opposed the law. Although 1028 prominent economists petitioned President HOOVER not to sign the bill he did so. The Act produced immediate foreign retaliation. Within two years 25 nations established high tariffs. This resulted in a further slump in American foreign trade.

Hawes-Cutting Act   Also known as the Hare-Hawes-Cutting Act and the Philippine Independence Act of 1933. A law of Congress enacted over President

84

HOOVER'S VETO in January, 1933 providing for the complete independence of the PHILIPPINE ISLANDS after a ten year period of political and economic tutelage. The Act was not to become effective unless its terms were approved by the Philippine legislature within one year. It immediately produced political conflict within the Islands between an element favoring its acceptance and a group which demanded immediate and complete independence. It was ultimately turned down by the Island legislature. In 1934 Congress renewed the offer of independence in the Tydings-McDuffie Act which became the basis for Philippine independence.

Heimwehr (Austrian) A militant organization formed in Austria in the 1920's. It was composed of agrarians who were bitterly opposed to the Socialist program of the Vienna proletariat. The original program of the organization called for the overthrow of the Socialists in Vienna and union with Germany. Steidle, Pfriemer, and Rüdiger von Starhemberg were the leaders. By 1931 the Heimwehr included 60,000 armed men. (By the Treaty of St. Germain, the Austrian army was limited to 30,000.)

Heligoland (Holy land) An island in the North Sea about forty miles from the mouth of the Elbe annexed to Germany in 1892. Of great strategic importance in World War I as an air and naval base. The Versailles Treaty stipulated the dismemberment of all the island's fortifications and its restoration as a bathing resort. However, Nazi Germany made Heligoland a fortress once more, only to have these fortifications razed by British troops which occupied it after the war. It is once more a popular German bathing resort.

Herriot, Édouard (1872-) French statesman. Born in Troyes. Mayor of Lyons (1905-24). Premier (1924-25, 1926, 1932). President of the Chamber of Deputies in the Vichy government (1942-45). Freed after liberation, he resumed leadership of the Radical Socialist Party. In 1947, he became president of the National Assembly. Author of *The United States of Europe* (1930) and a biography of Beethoven (Eng. tr. 1935).

Hess, Walther Richard Rudolf (1894-) Nazi leader. Born in Alexandria, Egypt. He took part in the Munich "BEER-HALL PUTSCH" of 1923 (q.v.) and was imprisoned with Hitler. While in prison he helped Hitler prepare *Mein Kampf*. In 1934 he was designated as deputy leader of the Nazi Party. In 1939 he was named third in order of succession after Hitler and Göring. In 1941, on the eve of the German invasion of Russia, he flew solo to Scotland where he pleaded ineffectually for a negotiated peace between England and Germany. He was held as a prisoner-of-war in England. In 1946 he was condemned to life imprisonment by the Nuremberg Tribunal.

Himmler, Heinrich (1900-45) Nazi police chief. Born in Munich. Flag-bearer in the "BEER-HALL PUTSCH" (1923) (q.v.). He organized the SS (1929) and soon made it a powerful force. In 1936 he became police chief. With his notorious secret police force (Gestapo) he unleashed an unmatched political and anti-Semitic reign of terror—first in Germany, then in war-occupied countries. In 1943 he was made Minister of Interior and was charged with crushing defeatism. In 1944 he became commander of the home army. In 1945 he made the offer of unconditional surrender to the British and Americans, but not the Russians. When the offer was rejected, he disappeared, but fell into British hands. After surrender of Germany, he committed suicide (1945).

Hindenburg, Paul von (in full Paul Ludwig Hans Anton von Beneckendorff und von Hindenburg). (1847-1934.) German general. President of the Weimar Republic. Born in Posen. Fought in the Austro-Prussian Wars. Member of the general staff (1877). Major general (1896). Lieutenant general (1900). Commanding general of the 4th corps (1903). Retired in 1911. Because of his knowledge of the defensive potentials of East Prussia, he was given command in the east in 1914. He won a complete victory over the Russians at TANNENBERG (1914) (q.v.). Rewarded by being made field marshal. He waged a successful campaign in Poland (1915). Chief of staff (1916). With Ludendorff he directed all German strategy (1917-18). Retired (1919). Elected president (1925-32). Re-elected (1932-34). Appointed Hitler chancellor (1933).

Hiroshima, bombing of The first military use of the ATOMIC BOMB. It was dropped on August 6, 1945 on Hiroshima, Japan, a military and naval center with a population of 350,000. Several square miles of buildings, representing three-fifths of the city, were demolished, and 135,000 casualties inflicted. These included 66,000 dead and 69,000 wounded.

Hitler, Adolf (1889-1945) German statesman. Born at Braunau, Upper Austria, the son of a customs official, he was originally named Schicklgruber. Orphaned early in life, he lived a life of hardship in Vienna. He held various jobs and read extensively in economics, history, etc. Becoming a draftsman, he migrated to Munich in 1912. He served honorably in the First World War, in which he was promoted to lance-corporal and decorated. In the post-war period, he attained, largely through persuasive oratory, leadership of the German National Socialist Party. Raising a semi-military organization, he attempted to seize control of the government through a *coup* (the "BEER-HALL PUTSCH," q.v.), 1923, but failed and was imprisoned for nine months, during which time he wrote *Mein Kampf.* After winning support of the large industrialists, he reorganized his party, now emphasizing anti-Semitism, anti-Marxism, and extreme nationalism. His party now attracted wide membership. Although

Hitler unsuccessfully opposed Hindenburg for the presidency in 1932, he was appointed chancellor early in 1933. By exploiting the REICHSTAG FIRE (q.v.) (Feb. 1933), he gained absolute control of the state. In June 1934 he "purged" the most notorious opposition within his party (see BLOOD PURGE). Upon the death of Hindenburg (Aug. 1934), he assumed the title of Reichsführer. He rearmed Germany (1935) and sent troops into the Rhineland. He formed the Rome-Berlin Axis with Mussolini (1936) and annexed Austria (1938). He secured the Sudetenland of Czechoslovakia (1938) and Bohemia and Moravia (1939). In 1939 he seized Memel from Lithuania. Upon Poland's refusal to surrender Danzig, he attacked Poland, thus beginning the Second World War. His armies rolled over Poland, Denmark, Norway, Holland, Belgium, France, Romania, Yugoslavia, and Greece. His armies penetrated deep into European Russia and across north Africa. Then the tide of victory turned at El Alamein (Oct. 1942) and Stalingrad (Nov. 1942). As the invading armies closed in on Berlin, Hitler is alleged to have taken his own life (May 1, 1945).

Ho Chi-Minh (1892-) Indo-Chinese revolutionary and statesman. He organized the Indo-Chinese resistance movement against the Japanese invaders (1941-1945). In 1945 he accepted the Japanese surrender as the head of Vietnam Republic. The Allies, after negotiating with Ho refused to recognize this government, backing instead, the Bao Dai government of South Vietnam. The Indo-Chinese civil war ensued, with the French-backed South Vietnamese government claiming Ho to be a communist puppet. An armistice was declared after the Geneva agreements (1954). Ho has been president of North Vietnam since 1945.

Holmes, Oliver Wendell, Jr. (1841-1935) Jurist. b. Boston. Graduated from Harvard (1861). Fought with Union Army in Civil War. Graduated from Harvard

Law school, 1866. Justice of Massachusetts Supreme Court. Appointed by Theodore Roosevelt to U.S. Supreme Court in 1902. He served until his retirement in 1932. Became the Court's most noted liberal and dissenter. He denounced the use of the Fourteenth Amendment to prevent the making of social experiments.

✗ **Hoover, Herbert Clark** (1874-) Thirty-first President of the United States. b. West Branch, Iowa. Graduated Stanford University as a mining engineer (1895); worked in the West and as a mining expert in Australia and other parts of the world; and as a gold-mining engineer in various places (1895-1913); chairman, American Relief Commission in London (1914-15); chairman, Commission for Relief in Belgium (1915-19); U.S. Food Administrator (1917-19); member, War Trade Council; chairman, U.S. Grain Corporation, Interallied Food Council; in charge of relief in countries of eastern Europe (1921); appointed by HARDING, U.S. Secretary of Commerce (1921-28); reappointed by COOLIDGE; elected President of the United States (1929-33); Stock Market Crash and the Depression resulted in difficult administration problems; Farm Relief Act, and Federal Farm Board secured through his efforts; created the Reconstruction Finance Corporation; ordered troops to evict Bonus Expeditionary Force from the capital (1932); denounced by liberal groups for his conservative domestic politics and his isolationist foreign policy; coordinator of food supply to 38 nations (1946); headed HOOVER COMMISSION of 12 men to study the reorganization of the executive branch of the government and recommended these reorganization plans to Congress; in opposition to TRUMAN's foreign policy. Author of *The Basis for Lasting Peace* (1945), and his autobiography in several volumes (1951 and 1952).

✗ **Hoover Moratorium** (1931) This was the suspension by President HOOVER of all Allied war debts to the U.S.

incurred as a result of World War I. The Allies had been hard-hit by the depression of the late 20's in Europe and felt incapable of continued payments. The debts were never, in fact, taken up again.

Horthy, Miklos von Nagybanya (1868-1957) Regent of Hungary (1920-44). Naval aide-decamp to Emperor Francis Joseph, he commanded the Austro-Hungarian fleet in 1918. He was captured by Americans in 1945. He was then released. He lives in retirement in a country home near Munich.

Hossbach Document (1937) This was Hitler's documented statement to the German General Staff of his pre-war plans to take over Czechoslovakia and Austria and to neutralize Poland.

Hughes, Charles Evans (1862-1948) Statesman and jurist. b. New York. Graduated from Brown University and Columbia Law School (1884). Corporation lawyer in New York City. Republican Governor of New York (1906-10). Noted as reforming governor. In 1910 he was appointed by President Taft to the U.S. Supreme Court, resigning in 1916 to campaign as Republican presidential candidate when he was narrowly defeated by WOODROW WILSON. Served as Secretary of State to Harding and Coolidge (1921-24), during which time he worked for disarmament and against recognition of Russia. Reappointed to the Supreme Court as Chief Justice by Hoover in 1930, he served until retirement in 1941.

Hull, Cordell (1871-1955) Statesman. b. Tenn. Graduated, Cumberland University (1891); admitted to the bar (1891); judge, 5th judicial circuit of Tennessee (1903-07); member, U.S. House of Representatives (1907-21; 1923-31); U.S. Senator (1931-33); author of federal Income Tax law (1913) and its revision (1916), and the federal estate and inheritance tax law (1916); appointed by ROOSEVELT U.S. Secretary of State (1933-44); negotiated Reciprocal Trade Agreements with Latin-American countries; awarded Nobel Peace Prize (1945). Author of autobiography *The Memoirs of Cordell Hull* (1948).

Human Rights Those rights defining the basic freedoms and liberties of human beings. As discussed by the members of the United Nations Human Rights Commission in 1952, human rights include freedom of religion, freedom of expression, the right to work, a decent living for all families, the right to social security, the right to housing, and the right of everyone to continuous improvement of living conditions. Some delegates argued that human rights legislation should include bars against racial and religious discrimination, abolition of segregation, the rights of labor to strike and picket, the outlawing of discrimination in employment because of political affiliation, and cultural freedom to pursue basic research and education in the sciences. On April 12, 1952 the United Nations Human Rights Commission convened in an attempt to conclude a six year old effort to define those basic freedoms which should be included in international pacts on human rights. Considerable conflict arose between small states and large states over a clause dealing with the autonomy rights of colonial dependencies. In the United States opposition was expressed by the American Bar Association and other groups to the Covenant on Human Rights because of the clauses dealing with labor, employment, and housing.

Hungarian Communist Government (1919) In 1919 the Hungarian Soviet Republic was set up after a revolution led by BELA KUN. A series of wars with Czechoslovakia and Romania led to the defeat of the communist government and to an uprising by anti-communist Hungarian forces. A dictatorship was set up (1920) with HORTHY as regent. Bela Kun fled to the USSR.

Hungarian Uprising (1956) In Oct. 1956 a general uprising occurred throughout Hungary against the communist-controlled government. A government was formed by Imre Nagy, which appealed to the United Nations for support and took Hungary out of the WARSAW PACT. Within a short time, Soviet troops overran the country, suppressing the revolution and establishing a Soviet-controlled government under Janos Kadar. Nagy was executed in 1958.

Hydrogen Bomb Popularly known as the H-bomb. On January 31, 1950 President TRUMAN announced that he had instructed the ATOMIC ENERGY COMMISSION to begin the production of the hydrogen bomb. On January 6, 1951 Congress authorized an appropriation of $1,000,000,000 to the Atomic Energy Commission for the construction of a plant at Aiken, South Carolina for work on the bomb. On April 2, 1952 the A.E.C. chairman disclosed a delay in building this plant because of inadequate priority ratings on military items. Although the power of the hydrogen bomb has not been officially revealed, it has been estimated that it will be 1,000 times more powerful than the Atomic Bomb which has the energy equivalent of 20,000 tons of TNT. In November, 1952, a Hydrogen Bomb was detonated on Eniwetok Atoll. It was the most devastating weapon ever developed.

I

Imperial Chancellor, German According to the constitution of the German Empire (1871-1918), the chancellor enjoyed a commanding position, so long as he retained the confidence of the Emperor. He was the active agent of the Emperor. By custom he was the head of the ministry of Prussia as well as chancellor. He presided over the Bundesrat and cast Prussia's 17 votes in that body. He might address the Reichstag whenever he wished. He proposed most of the laws for the empire and for Prussia. He appointed and supervised the heads of the imperial departments. He executed all imperial laws.

Imperial Conference (1926) A meeting of representatives of Britain and the dominions. This conference (among other things) adopted the Balfour Report which declared: "They (Great Britain and the dominions) are autonomous communities within the British Empire, equal in status, in no way subordinate one to another in any aspect of their domestic or external affairs, though united by a common allegiance to the Crown, and freely associated as members of the British Commonwealth of Nations." This declaration became law in Dec. 1931, when Parliament passed the Statute of Westminster.

India, Creation of the Independent Republic of The British rulers first gave a measure of independence to India in 1919 with the passage of the Government of India Act. It provided for native control at provincial levels of minor governmental functions such as agriculture and education. At the national level there was a bicameral advisory legislature underneath a British Viceroy and Council of State. The INDIAN NATIONAL CONGRESS led by GANDHI, rejected the government because of its limited nature, and instituted a series of civil disobedience campaigns. As a result of negotiation and the threat of revolution, the British government passed another Government of India Act (1935) to go into effect in 1937. It separated Burma and Aden from India and provided for wide autonomy at provincial levels, under appointed governors and elected legislatures. There was a bicameral legislature at the national level under the Governor-General, who controlled defense, foreign affairs, etc. In 1947, the British Parliament passed the Indian Independence Bill which gave independence to the states of India and Pakistan (a part of old India mainly populated by Moslems) on Aug. 15, 1947. Pakistan became a dominion, and India a republic. They are both a part of the BRITISH COMMONWEALTH. The Prime Minister of India since independence has been JAWAHARLAL NEHRU, the head of the major political party in the Indian National Congress. In the cold war India has pursued a neutralist course.

Indian National Congress Under British rule in India the Congress was a revolutionary group aiming at the Independence of India. After Independence the Congress assumed the role of a moderate socialist party. It has controlled a majority in the Indian legislature since the beginning of independent rule.

Indonesia, Creation of the Republic of the United States of At the end of World War II Japan surrendered to a Republic of the U.S. of Indonesia (created 1945), which, before occupation had been the Dutch East Indies. This government was accepted by the British and the American forces. The Netherlands, however, invaded (1945) the islands causing a civil war. The United Nations arranged an armistice in 1948. In 1949 at the Hague Conference, the Netherlands officially gave independence to Indonesia.

Inter-Allied Debts Eighteen days after the United States joined the belligerents in World War I, Congress passed an act which authorized the lending of 3 billion dollars to the Allies at 5% interest. Other loans were made during the war and in the immediate post-war period. Approximately $10,338,000,000 was loaned to 20 nations. Of this sum, $7,077,000,000 was loaned during the war and $3,261,000,000, or 31% after the armistice. Britain received 41% of the total; France, 33%; Italy, 16%. During the 1920's various debtor countries made funding arrangements with the United States. There was close correlation between what the debtor countries paid and what they received from Germany in the form of reparations, despite the vigorous attempts of the United States to divorce reparations from debt payment. When Germany stopped payment of reparations, all debtor countries, except Finland, stopped payments. In 1934, the United States passed a law forbidding defaulting nations to float loans in the United States. All told the borrowers repaid $2,628,000,000.

Inter-American Treaty of Reciprocal Assistance (1947) A hemispheric mutual defense treaty signed by all the American nations with the exception of Ecuador, Canada, and Nicaragua.

International Bank for Reconstruction and Development. Established December 27, 1945 when 28 nations signed Articles of Agreement drawn up at the BRETTON WOODS CONFERENCE of 1944. In 1952 there were 50 members. United States participation was authorized on July 31, 1945 and the Bank began operations on June 26, 1946. Of the subscribed capital of $8,438,500,000 the United States share totalled $3,175,000,000 or 37.63 percent of the total capital subscription. The Bank's purpose is to lend money for reconstruction in war torn areas and in underdeveloped countries and to guarantee government loans and loans from private agencies for such purposes. It also aims to promote long range balanced growth of international trade so that labor productivity and living standards may be improved. By 1952 the Bank had made 52 loans to 24 member countries totaling $1,326,000,000. Loans in 1950 and 1952 were granted to member nations for the purchase of airplanes and the development of electric power, railways, and ports. The largest loan was the sum of $250,000,000 to France in 1947, but only four have been greater than $40,000,000. Twenty-eight loans have been for $10,000,000 or less.

International Confederation of Free Trade Unions (I.C.F.T.U.) A confederation of trade unions of the world that are not communist-dominated. These unions represent approximately 51 million workers. In opposition is the communist-dominated World Federation of Trade Unions (W.F.T.U.).

International Court of Justice of the UN The International Court of Justice is similar to the Permanent Court of International Justice of the League of Nations. In fact, its Constitution is the same as its predecessor's. The principal difference is that UN members adhere to the court *automatically,* whereas in the League, membership was optional. The permanent seat of the Court is at the Hague, but it may hold its hearings elsewhere.

International Court of Justice See WORLD COURT.

International Labor Organization This body was created in 1919 by the Treaty of Versailles. Its purpose was to lay down equitable conditions for labor and to induce governments to take steps to incorporate these principles into their national legislation. The Organization works through an International Labor Office located in Geneva. General conferences were convened whenever there was a sufficient number of subjects for consideration. Sovereign states might be represented in these conferences by four delegates, one of whom should represent capital and one labor. States were at liberty to accept or reject the recommendations of these conferences. The International Labor Organization was in effect part of the League of Nations. Yet, it was independent from it. Non-League members (the United States, for example) might belong. When the UN was organized, the International Labor Organization became part of it. The ILO is now affiliated with the Economic and Social Council of the UN. Its headquarters are in Geneva, Switzerland.

International Monetary Fund. Established by 44 nations at the BRETTON WOODS CONFERENCE in July, 1944 and effective on December 27, 1945. By 1952, 49 nations had become members. The objectives of the fund were to promote international trade by insuring the stability of exchange rates, encourage international monetary cooperation, avoid competitive exchange devaluation, establish a system of multi-lateral payments in current transactions by eliminating restrictions, eliminate discriminatory currency arrangements, and to permit members to draw upon the resources of the Fund. The Fund's resources are provided by the payment of quotas by members in gold, United States dollars, or its own currency. In 1952, total quotas amounted to $8,036,000,000 of which the United States' subscription was $2,750,000,000. The United States exercises 30 percent of the voting control of the Fund. By 1950 it had extended loans totalling $794,900,000 to 19 countries. *See* INTERNATIONAL BANK FOR RECONSTRUCTION AND DEVELOPMENT.

International Refugee Organization Created 1948. It is an agency of the UNITED NATIONS concerned with the aid to, and resettlement of refugees. Refugees were a major consequence of the upheavals of World War II.

Internationale, Third The Third Internationale (Comintern) was founded informally by LENIN in Switzerland in 1917, officially organized in Moscow two years later. It supported the Marxian theory that capitalism would be overthrown by force because of its resistance to fundamental social changes. The comintern was abolished by Stalin (1943) in the interest of wartime harmony among the United Nations. It was revived in the form of the organization "Cominform," in 1947.

Invasion of the Ruhr (1923) French and Belgium troops invaded the Ruhr claiming that Germany was in default on reparations to the Allies.

Iraq, Independence of the Kingdom of Iraq was a province of Turkey until the Treaty of Sèvres, when it became a mandate of Great Britain. In 1932 Iraq became an independent state. In 1958 Iraq joined with Jordan to form the Arab Federal State of Iraq and Jordan under the Iraq King, Faisal II. In July, 1958 King Faisal was assassinated and Iraq was proclaimed a republic and the union with Jordan dissolved.

Iron Curtain A term coined by WINSTON CHURCHILL designating the barrier formed by the USSR and the Eastern European communist countries in regard to communication and travel into the communist countries.

Iron Guard A fascist pro-German organization of Romania. Under the leadership of General Antonescu, they forced King Carol to abdicate (1940). Thereupon, the Iron Guard set up a dictatorship for Romania which lasted until 1944, when it was overthrown by the conquering armies of the Soviet Union.

"Island-Hopping Campaign" The offensive effort of the United States Navy in World War II in the Pacific theater. It began with the invasion and capture of the SOLOMON ISLANDS in August, 1942 and was concluded with the invasion of the Japanese homeland after the atomic BOMBING OF HIROSHIMA and Nagasaki in 1945.

Israel, Creation of the State of The BALFOUR DECLARATION of the British government (1917), was a statement favoring the establishment of a national Jewish home in Palestine. The mandate of Palestine under Great Britain was the scene of violent Jewish-Arab incidents over the issue of Jewish immigration and a Jewish state. In 1937 the Peel Commission Report envisaged a division of Palestine into a Jewish state, an Arab state, and a small British mandate. It was accepted by the World Zionist Congress, rejected by the Pan-Arab Congress. During and after World War II Jewish and Arab military organization grew in

98

strength. The problem of a Jewish state was referred by the British to the UNITED NATIONS. In 1947 the GENERAL ASSEMBLY recommended the partition of Palestine into Jewish and Arab states. On May 14, 1948 the British mandate ended and the state of Israel was proclaimed. The ARAB ISRAELI WAR began the same day.

Istiqlal   Formed in 1943. It is a Moroccan party intent on the independence of No. Africa from France.

J

Japan, Occupation of   The POTSDAM DECLARATION of July 26, 1945 set down the terms of the Japanese surrender. Among other provisions it declared that Japan would be occupied by Allied forces until the objectives of DISARMAMENT, REPARATIONS, territorial transfer, and punishment of war criminals would be achieved. The surrender terms established on September 2, 1945 provided that Japan must accept the provisions of the Potsdam Declaration and that "the authority of the Emperor and the Japanese Government to rule the state shall be subject to the Supreme Commander for the Allied Powers." On August 14, 1945 General MACARTHUR was appointed Supreme Commander as head of Allied Occupation forces in Japan. A Far Eastern Commission, consisting of representatives of Australia, Burma, Canada, China, Great Britain, France, India, Holland, New Zealand, Pakistan, the PHILIPPINES, the Soviet Union, and the United States, was established. The Commission was authorized to form the policies, principles, and standards by which Japan's obligations under the surrender terms would be fulfilled. It was authorized to review directives issued to SCAP and all actions taken by the latter within the Commission's jurisdiction. The Allied Council for Japan was established to advise and consult with SCAP in carrying out the surrender terms and the policies approved by the Commission. The Council consisted of the United States' member of SCAP, a member from China and from the Soviet Union, and a member representing jointly the United Kingdom, New Zealand, and India. In 1946 General MacArthur ordered the Japanese cabinet to carry out a series of political PURGES. In July 1947 the United States suggested a conference of the 11 members of the Far Eastern Commission to consider a peace settlement for Japan. All member nations, except the Soviet Union, accepted the proposal. The latter insisted that the treaty be prepared by the four-power Council of Foreign Ministers. On April 11, 1951 General MacArthur was replaced by General Ridgway as the Supreme Commander for the Allied Powers. During the occupation political, economic, and social reforms were undertaken. The Japanese government was democratized, with sovereignty transferred from the Emperor to the popularly elected House of Representatives (Diet). The school curriculum was simplified and purged of militarist and chauvinist nuances. Repatriation of war prisoners was almost completed. The dissolution of the business and financial monopolies was effected, with voting rights taken over by a government commission which seized securities of the *Zaibatsu* families, for resale to the public. Between 1946 and 1949 reparations in the form of industrial products were delivered until, in the latter year, the United States declared its opposition to further reparations. On May 1, 1951 General Ridgway announced the relaxation of occupation directives. On September 8, 1951 a treaty of peace with Japan was signed at San Francisco by the United States and 48 other nations.

Japanese Peace Treaty A treaty signed at San Francisco on September 8, 1951 between Japan and 49 nations including the United States. The representatives of the Soviet Union, Poland, and Czechoslovakia attended the peace conference, but refused to sign. The provisions of the treaty ended the state of war among the signatories, recognized the full sovereignty of Japan and its right to apply for UNITED NATIONS membership, and established Japanese renunciation of all rights to Formosa, the Pescadores, the Kuriles, Sakhalin, and all the islands formerly mandated to Japan by the LEAGUE OF NATIONS. It further provided for Japanese agreement to U.N. TRUSTEESHIP over the Ryukyu Islands, the Bonins, and several other islands. It required Japan to agree to peaceful settlement of international disputes, and provided for the continued occupation of Japan until 90 days after the treaty had been ratified by a majority of the signatories. The Treaty also provided for Fisheries, Tariff, and maritime relations among the signatories, and for the payment by Japan of REPARATIONS through manufactured goods. Japan agreed to recognize the industrial, literary, and artistic property rights of the signatory nations in Japan and to indemnify war prisoners with claims against the Japanese government. The United States Senate ratified the Treaty on March 20, 1952.

Johnson Debt Default Act (April 13, 1934) Prohibited loans to any foreign government in default to the U.S. Token payments were continued up to December, 1933. On June 15, 1934, Britain, Italy, Czechoslovakia and all other debtors defaulted with the exception of Finland who continued to meet her payments in full.

This new approach to neutrality, proposed by isolationist Senator Hiram Johnson of California sought to disentangle U.S. economic interests from foreign controversies.

Jones Act Passed by Congress in 1916. The law provided a civil government for the PHILIPPINE ISLANDS. It conferred Philippine citizenship upon all inhabitants in the Islands who were Spanish subjects on April 11, 1899 and their descendants, and granted the franchise to all literate male citizens over 21 years of age. It established an elective bi-cameral legislature consisting of a Senate and House of Representatives to replace the Philippine Commission. The justices of the insular Supreme Court were to be appointed by the President of the United States.

K

Kaganovich, Lazar Moiseyevich (1893-) Soviet revolutionary and statesman. A First Vice-Chairman of the Soviet Council of Ministers.

Kapp Putsch March 13-17, 1920. An attempt by a group of German monarchists, headed by Wolfgang Kapp, to secure control of the nation through a *coup d'état*. The Kapp forces seized the government buildings in Berlin, while the government fled to Stuttgart. The movement collapsed as a result of a general strike by trade unionists.

Karl Marx Hof Municipal houses built for workmen in Vienna by the Socialist government. Completed in 1930, the project was the largest dwelling house in

Europe, being more than three-fifths of a mile long and containing almost 1400 apartments. Converted into a fort by the Schutzbund, a semi-military workers' organization, it was besieged (Feb. 11-15, 1934) when the government under Dollfuss crushed the Socialist Party. Many units of the Hof were ruined by artillery fire. Since the end of World War II, the Hof has been rebuilt.

Kellogg, Frank B. (1856-1937) Diplomat. b. Potsdam, N. Y. Common school education. Admitted to bar (1877). Special counsel for U.S. against Standard Oil Company. Appointed ambassador to Great Britain (1924). Secretary of State in Coolidge Cabinet (1925-9). Judge of Permanent Court of International Justice (1930-35). Awarded Nobel Peace Prize in 1929 for his work on the Kellogg-Briand Pact (q.v.).

Kellogg-Briand Pact Also known as Pact of Paris and Pact of Peace. A series of treaties reciprocally negotiated by 15 states in 1928 in which the signatory nations agreed to renounce war as an instrument of national policy. Its significance lies in its pioneer effort to secure an international affirmation of the renunciation of war despite its material failures in preventing subsequent outbreaks of hostilities. The idea of the pact was first broached to Secretary of State Frank B. Kellogg by the French foreign minister Aristide Briand as a bi-lateral agreement. Upon the suggestion of Kellogg the treaty was expanded to include the other 13 nations. Subsequently, most of the world adhered to the Pact, some with reservations.

Kenyatta, Jomo (1893-) Kenya revolutionary. President of the Kenya African Union (1947-).

Kerala A territory on the southwest coast of India which is India's only Communist-run state. Kerala's governor is E. M. S. Namboodiripad, a Brahmin who believes that Communism can operate within India's constitutional guarantees. Capital of the state is Trivandrum. Kerala produces more than 90% of India's rubber, half its tea and monopolizes its pepper and cashew exports.

Kerensky, Alexander (1881-) Russian revolutionary leader. He joined the Labor Party, although he really was a member of the Social Revolutionary Party. He was made minister of justice in the Provisional Government (1917) which was set up after the abdication of the czar. Later (July 1917), he succeeded Prince Lvov as premier. He was overthrown by the Bolshevik revolution (Nov. 1917). He now resides in the United States.

Khaki Elections British elections held in December, 1918. In these elections, Lloyd George appealed to the people to support the wartime coalition on its record. He promised that William II of Germany would be tried as a war criminal and that Germany would be assessed large indemnities. He promised to protect "essential" industries and to take measures to prevent the dumping of foreign goods. He also promised to care for the veterans, settle the Irish Question, and reform the House of Lords. During the campaign the coalition was deserted by some Liberals and Conservatives and all Laborites. Nevertheless the coalition captured two-thirds of the seats in Commons.

Khrushchev, Nikita Sergeyevich (1894-) Soviet statesman. Fought in the war against the counter-revolutionaries (1921). Member of the Supreme Soviet (1937). First Secretary of the Ukrainian Communist party (1938). Led the resistance of the Ukrainian underground during the German occupation of World War II. First Secretary of the Communist party after the death of Stalin (1953). Denounced the "cult of personality" as embodied by Stalin, to the Communist Party Congress (1956). He solidified his power in 1957 with the downgrading of MOLOTOV and MALENKOV, and in 1958 made himself premier, replacing Bulganin.

Komsomol The Communist Youth Movement. It is a training organization for future Communist Party members. It contains the elite of the Russian nation.

Korea, Creation of the Republic of When the American occupation of South Korea came to an end, an election was held under United Nations auspices. A constitution was accepted and the Republic of Korea created (Aug. 15, 1948) with SYNGMAN RHEE as its President. A third of the population and half of the territory of Korea remained under Soviet control. It was subsequently changed into the DEMOCRATIC PEOPLE'S REPUBLIC OF KOREA.

Korean War At the Cairo Conference Roosevelt, Churchill, and Chiang Kai-Shek declared that Korea should be "free and independent." At the POTSDAM CONFERENCE the 38th parallel was designated as the dividing line between the Soviet and American occupations of Korea. In August, 1945 Soviet and United States troops entered Korea. In December, 1945 Secretary of State James F. Byrnes, Foreign Minister Ernest Bevan, and Foreign Minister V. M. Molotov agreed to a five year TRUSTEESHIP over Korea to be administered by the three powers. On Aug. 15, 1948 the Republic of Korea was established below the 38th parallel. The People's Democratic Republic of Korea was established in North Korea Sept. 9, 1948. The inability of the major powers to reconcile their political conflicts, the "COLD WAR," the division of Korea, and the internal political struggle within Korea formed the background of the war, which began when the North Korean Army crossed the 38th parallel on June 25, 1950. Two days later President TRUMAN ordered General MACARTHUR to come to the aid of South Korea and the SECURITY COUNCIL ordered resistance to the invasion. On July 8 President Truman named MacArthur as the UNITED NATIONS commander-in-chief. The United States 7th Fleet was ordered to FORMOSA to prevent an attack on or from it. The first three months of the fighting witnessed a steady UN retreat into South Korea until its forces held, in September, behind the Naktong River. The diversionary action which resulted in the capture of Inchon on September 15 led to a counter-offensive which brought the UN Army within sight of the Manchurian border at the Yalu River. On November 24th General MacArthur opened a major offensive with 100,000 troops. On November 26th a Chinese force, estimated at 200,000 crossed the Yalu River. By January 1, 1951 the combined Chinese-North Korean Army had reached the 38th parallel once more. Here, fighting within 70 miles north and south of the parallel continued at a stalemate for the next six months. Attempts at negotiating an end to the war began in January, 1951 with the demand by the Chinese Communists for a seat in the United Nations. In the ensuing months charges and counter-charges were made by the belligerents and on February 1, 1951 the General Assembly voted Communist China an aggressor. The months of bickering, accusations, and interruptions finally culminated in the opening of armistice negotiations on July 10th in which Admiral Charles T. Joy was named the UN negotiator and General Nam Il the North Korean negotiator. For the next year limited ground and air action went on as the negotiations proceeded with bitter accusations made by the negotiators against each other. An Armistice was finally signed in July, 1953. United States casualties totalled 137,051 while those of Korea were estimated as high as 1,312,836. Of these totals the U.S. dead and missing were reported to be 33,559 and Korea, 875,000.

Kotelawala, Sir John Lionel (1897-)   Ceylonese statesman. Prime Minister of Ceylon (1953-56).

Kun, Béla (1885-?)   Hungarian communist. Born in Transylvania, he was a journalist and soldier. Captured by the Russians in 1915, he embraced communism and returned to Hungary (March, 1919) to set up a communistic republic. This collapsed in August, 1919. Kun then returned to Russia, where he may still be living. Rumor has it that he perished in the purges of the 1930's.

Kuomintang   The revolutionary party of China under Sun Yat-Sen. It is now the only political party of the Nationalist Chinese government on FORMOSA.

L

Labor Front, German   To replace labor unions which had been abolished in 1933, and employers associations, which were dissolved in 1934, a German Labor Front was set up by the Nazis. Headed by Dr. Robert Ley, this body was designed to coordinate all German workers and employers, both intellectual and manual. (In 1939 the Front had 30 million members.) It served as an apparatus for indoctrination of Nazi principles. It had some power to arbitrate labor disputes. Affiliated with it was a recreational organization, "Strength through Joy," which arranged cheap vacations for workers and their families.

Labor Party, British   When Joseph Chamberlain left the Liberal Party (1886), the labor vote was left completely stranded. In 1899, a general trade-union congress, held in London, formed a Labor Representation Committee, which sought to secure representation in Parliament. Angered by the Taff Vale Decision (1901), the Labor Representation Committee joined with the Fabian Socialists, the Social Democratic Federation, and the Independent Labor Party (1906) to form the Labor Party. The Labor Party has had three ministries: 1924 (Ramsay MacDonald); 1929-31 (Ramsay MacDonald); and 1945-51 (Clement Attlee).

Laissez-Faire A French phrase originating among the Physiocrats in the 18th century. Literally translated it means "let do," and has been applied to the principle of the FREE ENTERPRISE System, having come to mean a hands-off policy by government with respect to business operation. The doctrine presupposes the existence of natural economic laws of the market place which control the buying and selling of commodities, and assumes the existence of unfettered competition.

Lansing, Robert (1864-1928) Statesman. b. Watertown, New York. Graduated from Amherst College, 1886. Counsel for U.S. in various international questions. Succeeded William Jennings Bryan as Secretary of State in the Wilson cabinet in June, 1915 and continued in office throughout the war resigning in 1920. He was chosen to accompany Wilson and assist him in the peace negotiations in Paris, 1919.

Lansing-Ishii Agreement An agreement between the United States and Japan which was negotiated on November 2, 1917 for the purpose of adjusting the antagonistic claims of these parties in the Far East. The agreement affirmed the Open-Door Policy and the territorial integrity of China. The United States recognized Japan's special interests in China but refused to agree that this acknowledgement applied to MANCHURIA. Japan subsequently insisted that the United States had extended this recognition, and the latter country was denounced by the Chinese for its

108

alleged renunciation of the open-door policy. As a result of the negotiations at the WASHINGTON NAVAL CONFERENCE, a subsequent exchange of notes on March 30, 1923 provided for the mutual understanding of both nations that the Lansing-Ishii Agreement was abrogated.

Lateran Accord, The (Feb. 11, 1929) An agreement between the papacy and the Italian government ending the ROMAN QUESTION. It contained the following: 1. The pope was recognized as an independent sovereign. A state, called Vatican City, was created in which the pope was the sole sovereign. 2. In the future, Roman Catholicism was to be the sole religion of the state. Bishops were to be selected by the Church, but all nominees for bishoprics must first be cleared by the state. Bishops were required to swear loyalty to the king and state. All clerical salaries were to be paid by the state. The state would assist in enforcing canon law. Marriage was recognized as a sacrament and a religious ceremony was to be sufficient. Religious instruction was made compulsory in both elementary and secondary schools. 3. Italy consented to pay an immediate cash indemnity of $39,-375,000 and $52,500,000 in 5% bonds. This money was to indemnify the papacy for the events of 1870.

Lausanne, Treaty of (1923) A settlement which revised the TREATY OF SÈVRES. Turkey gave up claims to all non-Turkish territory. It received eastern Thrace and the Islands of Imbros and Tenedos. Greece surrendered Smyrna, but received all of the Aegean Islands except the two just mentioned. Italy retained the Dodecanese Islands and England Cyprus. The Straits were demilitarized. Turkey and Greece exchanged populations. In accordance with this last provision, about 350,000 Turks migrated from Greek territory; but over one million Greeks were expelled from Turkey.

Laval, Pierre (1883-1945) French politician. Born at Châteldon. Lawyer, deputy (1914), senator (1926), premier (1931-32, 1935-36). Originally a socialist, he eventually became a rightist. He became Petain's deputy (1940) and prime minister of the Vichy government (1942-45). He was condemned to death as a collaborationist with the Nazis and executed in 1945.

Law, Andrew Bonar (1858-1923) British statesman. Born in New Brunswick, Canada, he migrated to Scotland while still a boy. He was a Member of Parliament from 1900 for the Conservatives. Secretary of state for colonies (1915-16); chancellor of exchequer (1916-18); lord of the privy seal (1919-21); prime minister (1922-23).

League of Nations (1919-46) An international organization created by the TREATY OF VERSAILLES (1919). The main function of the League was the preservation of peace. The original members of the League were named in the Covenant, or constitution, of the League. Any fully self-governing state was eligible for membership if approved by a 2/3 vote of the League Assembly. Both Germany and Russia were excluded from the original list; but both subsequently became members. Germany resigned in 1933 at the time that Japan resigned because of the Manchurian affair. Russia was expelled from the League following its attack on Finland in 1939. Sixty countries were members of the League at one time or another. At the outbreak of the Second World War there were 46 members. The United States never joined. The League was administered by three major bodies: the Assembly, the Council, and the Secretariat. The Assembly consisted of representatives of all member countries. Each country had one vote. The Assembly convened for the first time on Nov. 15, 1920. Its last session adjourned Dec. 14, 1939. The Assembly might consider any matter within the sphere of action of the

League or affecting the peace of the world. The Assembly became an international forum. The League Council became a quasi-executive body. It was composed of permanent and elective members. The Council varied in size from 8 to 16. The first meeting took place Jan. 16, 1920. The last (107th meeting) closed Dec. 14, 1939. The Secretariat, or "civil service," of the League consisted of a Secretary-General and a staff of assistants. The Secretariat was divided into sections: mandates, health, minorities, etc. The Secretariat registered and published all treaties submitted to it. The Permanent Court of International Justice (World Court) and the International Labor Organization were constituted under terms of the League Covenant. On the threat of war, the League was to take action to safeguard the peace. After suitable investigation established the aggressor, the members of the League might impose an economic boycott against the offending member (*see* SANCTIONS). Should economic sanctions fail to halt the aggressor, military force might be used. This last step was never used. About 40 minor disputes were settled by the League, 20 of which might easily have led to war. However, the League failed signally to halt aggression committed by a major nation. The League's principal successes lay in health and social work. It helped Russian, Greek, and Armenian refugees. It administered mandated colonies, and the Saar and Danzig. The League formally came to an end Aug. 1, 1946, at which time its properties and other assets in Geneva, the seat of the League, were turned over to the United Nations. In Dec. 1946, the General Assembly of the United Nations accepted agreements whereby eight former League mandates would be transferred to the United Nations trusteeship system.

Lend Lease Act Passed by Congress in March, 1941. It conferred upon the President the power to lend or lease any equipment to any nation whose defense he considered necessary to the defense of the United States. Under the Act and its renewals over $50,000,-000,000 was extended to the allies of the United States in World War II by the end of 1945. Of this amount more than 60 percent went to Great Britain and about 22 percent to the Soviet Union. Approximately half of lend lease was in munitions and petroleum products, about one fifth in industrial commodities, and the rest in food and services. As provided in the law "reverse lend lease" accounted for much needed raw materials, food, and quarters for American troops abroad, the total valued at $17,000,000,000. Although nominally in the form of loans and/or rentals, this aid has in effect become, and probably was understood to be, open subsidies to those nations assisting the United States prior to and during World War II.

Lenin, Nikolai (real name **Vladimir Ilyich Ulyanov**) (1870-1924). Russian revolutionary and statesman. First practiced law in Samara (1892). Moved to St. Petersburg in 1894 where he began Socialist propaganda work. Arrested (1895). Exiled (1897) to eastern Siberia where he wrote *The Development of Capitalism in Russia*. Moved to Switzerland in 1900 and founded *Iskra* (the Spark), a revolutionary journal. Encouraged revolution during the Russo-Japanese War. Advocated "defeatism" at the start of World War I. Laid the foundations for the Third Internationale in 1915. Came to Russia in April 1917, and assumed leadership of the revolutionaries. Overthrew the government of Kerensky (Nov. 7, 1917). Became premier following the dissolution of the constituent assembly at his motion (Jan. 7, 1918). Established the dictatorship of the proletariat. Fought against counter-revolutionaries (1918-21). Established far-reaching reforms, later (1921) modified by the NEP. Died at Gorki (Jan. 21, 1924). His body has been embalmed and is on permanent exhibition in Moscow.

Leyte Gulf, Battle of The greatest naval battle of history. It was fought between the United States and Japanese navies in three engagements October 22-27, 1944, and resulted in the destruction of Japanese naval power. In the three battles in Surigao Strait, off Samar, and off Cape Engano, the United States employed 166 ships and 1280 planes against 65 Japanese ships and 716 planes. American losses during these battles and the subsequent Philippine campaign were 27 ships and 967 planes. The Japanese during this period, suffered casualties of five carriers, four battleships, 14 cruisers, and 43 other vessels, and an estimated 7,000 planes.

Liberal Party, British Although the British Whigs won a major victory by securing the passage of the Reform Bill of 1832, many of their leaders felt that the party needed a new name and a new direction if it was to survive. The old Whigs had been just as aristocratic as the Tories, being dominated by a group of wealthy peers. After 1832, many wealthy iron and cotton manufacturers entered the party. They wished to be thought of as a liberal, reforming element. In time, the Whig Party became known as the Liberal Party, since it espoused any "liberal" idea which was current among the bourgeoisie. The Liberal Party was a major force in England until 1920.

Liberia It is a Negro republic whose population of 1,600,000 occupies an area of 43,000 square miles. It was first settled in 1822, six years after Congress conferred a charter upon the American Colonization Society, authorizing it to transport emancipated slaves to the west African coast. Its independence was officially proclaimed in 1847. In 1942 and 1944 treaties between Liberia and the United States permitted the latter to establish troops, airports, and military and naval bases in Liberia. The nation's major enterprise is the million acre rubber concession granted to the

113

Firestone Plantations Company in 1925. An iron ore concession has been developed by the Republic Steel Corporation. Its principal crops are coffee, rice, and sugar cane. The city of Monrovia is the capital and chief port.

Libya, Creation of An Italian protectorate (1912-1943) it was given independence in 1951 by the United Nations General Assembly. There is a king with a partially elected bicameral legislature.

Lima, Declaration of The statement of the Eighth Pan-American Conference which met in Lima, Peru in 1938. At this meeting the Monroe Doctrine was made multilateral instead of unilateral in its enforcement. The Declaration further adopted resolutions proclaiming the members' will for peace, their sentiment of humanity and tolerance, their adherence to the principles of international law, their belief in the equal sovereignty of states, and their belief in individual liberty without religious or racial basis. The sentiments expressed in these resolutions were strengthened by subsequent reciprocal trade agreements and the exchange of cultural and educational facilities.

Little Entente, The An agreement between Czechoslovakia, Romania, and Yugoslavia with the encouragement and support of France. This alliance was an attempt to forestall a resurgence of the former Austro-Hungarian Empire. A formal agreement was signed at Belgrade (May 21, 1929) after bilateral treaties among the three powers had been in effect for nearly nine years. When Germany seized Czechoslovakia in 1939, the Little Entente came to an end.

Litvinov, Maxim Soviet communist leader and statesman. After the Russian revolution (1917) he represented the Soviet government in London. He signed the Kellogg Pact for the USSR (1928). He was the People's Commissar for foreign affairs (1930-39). During his term in office he strove for cooperation between the USSR and other countries. When he was superseded by Molotov (1939), the change marked a radical departure in Soviet foreign policy from internationalism to nationalism. He was Soviet Ambassador to the U.S. (1941-43).

Litvinov Nonaggression Treaties A series of treaties between the USSR and Finland, Estonia, Latvia, Lithuania, Poland, France, Romania, Turkey, Iran, and Afghanistan (1933). They were put forth by the Soviet Foreign Minister MAXIM LITVINOV, in order to secure alliances against German aggression.

Lloyd George, David (1863-1945) British statesman. Born in Manchester of Welsh parents. Studied law. Solicitor (1884). M.P. (1890). President of the Board of Trade (1905-08). Chancellor of the exchequer (1908-15). Minister of Munitions (1915-16). War Secretary (1916). Coalition Prime Minister and virtual dictator (1916-22). He carried England to victory in World War I. He played a large part in the peace settlements at the end of the war and negotiations which resulted in the creation of the Irish Free State.

Locarno Conference and Treaties (Oct. 5-16, 1925) Delegates from Germany, France, Britain, Belgium, Poland, and Czechoslovakia drew up several treaties to preserve the peace of Europe (signed Dec. 1). (1) A treaty of mutual guarantee of the Franco-German and Belgo-German frontiers (signed by France, Germany, Belgium, Britain and Italy). (2) Arbitration treaties between Germany and Poland and Germany and Czechoslovakia. (3) Arbitration treaties between Germany and Belgium and Germany and France. (4) Treaties between France and Poland and France and Czechoslovakia for mutual assistance in case of attack by Germany. Should violation of these treaties occur, the League Council was responsible for settlement.

The treaties were to go into effect when Germany entered the League of Nations, which it did in 1926.

Lodge, Henry Cabot (1850-1924) Statesman, author. b. Boston, and graduated from Harvard Law School in 1875. Represented Massachusetts in Congress 1887-93. From 1894 until his death he was the Senator from Massachusetts, serving as floor leader and chairman of the important Foreign Relations Committee. He was a partisan Republican, an imperialist and an isolationist after Wilson adopted the collective security plan of a League of Nations. Lodge is usually blamed for the parliamentary maneuvering and planning which resulted in the defeat of the Versailles Treaty and League Covenant in 1919 and 1920.

London Economic Conference Technically called the World Monetary and Economic Conference. A Conference in London in June and July, 1933 convened for the purpose of halting the world depression through international financial and economic agreement. Commodity agreements were negotiated by silver and wheat producing nations, but attempts at bringing about currency stabilization and tariff reduction failed. Belgium, France, Holland, and Switzerland, still on the Gold Standard, refused to discuss tariff reduction until agreement could be reached on currency stabilization. Governed by strong nationalist sentiment the United States refused to discuss the issue of war debts or to cooperate in international currency stabilization. While the Conference was still in session, President F. D. ROOSEVELT requested the recall of the American delegation, basing his decision on the thinking that the United States could extricate itself from the world depression by itself. The Conference failed to solve these fundamental problems.

London Naval Conference (Jan. 21-Apr. 22, 1930) Great Britain, the United States, France, Italy, and Japan met to consider the problems of extending the Wash-

116

ington Naval Disarmament Treaty and of limiting types of warcraft not included in the Washington Treaty. France and Italy did not sign the really vital parts of the pact, since France was determined to have the largest navy of any continental European nation, and Italy wished parity with France. Britain, Japan, and the United States settled the problems of cruisers and destroyers by compromise (10-6-10 ratio). The three powers were to have parity in submarines. No new capital ships were to be laid down until 1936. Aircraft-carrier figures remained the same as in the Washington Treaty: 135,000 tons each for Britain and the United States; 81,000 tons for Japan. An "escalator" clause permitted each signatory to increase tonnage in any category if, in its opinion, national security was endangered by new construction on the part of any nonsignatory.

London Naval Conference of 1936 A conference of the United States, Great Britain, Italy, France, and Japan from December, 1935 to March, 1936. It was convened to discuss the problems raised by the Japanese denunciation in December, 1934, of the Washington Naval Treaty. Upon the refusal of the United States and Great Britain to recognize Japan's claim to parity the latter withdrew from the conference. In the two power pact of March 25, 1936, England and the United States agreed to exchange data on their naval construction programs. They also agreed to limit certain types of warships but to set aside these limits in the event of war or if they were exceeded by a nonsignatory power. No provisions were contained for a quantitative limitation. As a result of inability to secure information from Japan about its naval construction program the two signatories agreed in 1938 to remove the limit of 35,000 tons for capital ships.

London, Secret Treaty of (April 26, 1915) Between Italy, France, Russia, and Great Britain. Under the terms

117

of this treaty, Italy agreed to join the Allies within a month in return for the following concessions: Italy was to receive (1) Trentino, Trieste, and all of south Tyrol. (2) Gorizia, Gradisca, Istria, and the islands of the Gulf of Quarnero. (3) Northern Dalmatia. (4) A protectorate over Valona and its hinterland (5) The Dodecanese Islands. (6) A sphere of influence in Asiatic Turkey. (7) An extension of its African colonies, if France and England should annex the German African colonies. (8) A war loan. (9) A promise that the papacy would not be supported in any diplomatic action taken contrary to the wishes of the Italian government.

Ludendorff, Erich Friedrich Wilhelm (1865-1937) German general. At the outbreak of World War I, he was made quartermaster-general. He worked with Hindenburg to defeat Russia. He engineered the collapse of Serbia and Romania. He planned the campaign which led to the defeat of the Italians at Caporetto. His plan of attack in 1918 nearly defeated the Allies. He fled to Sweden at the end of the war and then (1919) took up residence in Munich. He worked with Hitler in the early days of the Nazi movement. He later broke with Hitler and became an ardent pacifist.

Lusitania, Sinking of (May 7, 1915) The Lusitania, a British Cunard Liner, was torpedoed seven miles off the southeastern coast of Ireland by a German submarine. Almost 1200 lives were lost, including those of more than 100 Americans. Before this act, public opinion in the United States had been largely neutral or anti-British. Now it became strongly anti-German. The sinking of the Lusitania was the most important single event which caused the United States to declare war on the Central Powers.

Luxemburg, Rosa (1870-1919) German socialist agitator. Associated with Karl Liebknecht in the Spartacist movement. She was involved with him in the Sparta-

118

cist insurrection (1919). She was arrested with him and killed by army officers while being taken to prison.

Lytton Report (Oct. 4, 1932) In Sept., 1931 Japanese Army leaders launched an attack on major Manchurian cities which were occupied, completing Japanese domination of South Manchuria by January, 1932. In February, 1932, Japan formally recognized the new puppet state of Manchukuo. On Dec. 10, 1931, the League appointed the Lytton Commission to investigate the Manchurian crisis. The Committee's report stated that Japan's actions "were not in self-defense" although it admitted that the Japanese had a real problem on their hands in protecting their life and property in Manchuria. The Report condemned Japan but proposed a settlement recognizing Japan's special interest in Manchuria, which was to become an autonomous state under Chinese sovereignty but Japanese control. The Report was adopted by the League unanimously on Feb. 24, 1933 and on March 27, Japan gave notification of withdrawal from the League. The League could not recommend sanctions against Japan, it said, since no declaration of war had been made by either party in the "Shanghai incident." The League's moral force was broken on this issue.

M

MacArthur, Douglas (1880-) Army officer. b. Arkansas. Graduated, U.S.M.A., West Point (1903); member of general staff in France during World War I; commanded 42nd division (called the Rainbow division)

(1918-19); brigadier general; superintendent at West Point (1921-22); major general (1925); commanded Philippine Department (1928); general and chief of staff, U.S. Army (1930-35); director of organization of national defense for the Philippine government (1935-37) retired; recalled to service (1941) as lieutenant general and placed in command of the U.S. forces in the Far East; general (1941) supreme commander of Allied forces in the Southwest Pacific (1942); 5 star general (1944); launched Philippine campaign from Australia (October, 1944-July, 1945); accepted Japanese surrender in Tokyo (September, 1945); appointed Supreme Commander for Allied Powers in Japan (1945-1951); named commander of UN forces resisting North Korea (June, 1950); dismissed from Korean and Japanese posts (1951) because of differences with President TRUMAN; on inactive list (1951); named keynoter of Republican Nominating Convention (July, 1952); unsuccessful "Dark Horse" candidate for Republican presidential nomination (1952).

Mackensen, August von (1849-1945) German field marshal. He commanded the invasion of Poland (1914-15) and Romania (1916).

Madagascar Oct. 14, 1958 declared itself an autonomous republic within the French community.

Maginot Line A series of forts built by France along the Franco-German frontier to prevent Germany from invading France. Since the western end of the line ended at the Belgian frontier, it was fairly simple for the Germans to outflank the line by attacking France through Belgium. Although the Maginot line was said to be impregnable, events proved otherwise. The Germans broke through it in 1940. In 1944 when it was in the possession of the Germans, the Americans broke through it.

Magsaysay, Ramon (1907-1957)   Filipino statesman. President of the Philippine Republic 1953-57.

Malenkov, Georgi Maximilianovich (1902-)   Soviet statesman. Chairman of the Council of Ministers of the USSR (1953-55). He became the Minister of electric power stations in 1955.

Manchukuo   See MANCHURIA.

Manchuria   The former Manchu state in eastern Asia which is bounded on the east by Siberia and Korea, on the south by China, and on the west by China, Siberia, and Mongolia. Manchuria was invaded by Japan in 1931 and wrested from China. It was proclaimed an independent nation on February 18, 1932 and renamed Manchukuo by the Japanese on March 1, 1932. The interest of the United States in this territory was first manifested in Secretary of State Hay's "Open Door" notes in September-November, 1899. The Treaty of Portsmouth in 1905, Root-Takahira Agreement in 1908, Taft-Knox proposal of 1909-1910, LANSING-ISHII NOTES of 1917, and Nine Power Treaty of 1922 were subsequent expressions of continuing interest of this country in the sovereignty and independence of China. After the creation of Manchukuo Secretary of State Stimson proclaimed the doctrine of non-recognition on January 7, 1932. Up to World War II the United States abided by the STIMSON DOCTRINE. At the close of the war Manchuria was returned to China under its original name.

Mandate system   Begun in 1919. A system set up by Article 22 of the Covenant of the League of Nations for the administration of the former German colonies and the non-Turkish portions of the Ottoman Empire. These territories were divided among the Allied powers at the end of World War I. By this system, the Allied powers shared sovereignty over the mandates with the League of Nations. The mandates fell into three classes. Class A consisted of Iraq, Syria, Palestine, Lebanon, and Transjordan. It was believed that these countries could soon achieve independence. Today, they are all independent. Class B mandates included the Cameroons, Tanganyika, Togoland, and Ruanda. It was thought that considerable time would elapse before these countries could be self-governing. Class C consisted of Southwest Africa, German Samoa, New Guinea, and many islands in the Pacific. In these mandates, self-government is more remote than in the Class B group. With the creation of the UN, the mandates became Trust Colonies, and are administered by the Trusteeship Council of the UN. Mandates formerly under Japan are now administered by the United States.

Maniu, Iuliu (1873-) Romanian politician, head of the Peasant Party. Premier (1928-30, 1932-33), he endeavored to introduce liberal reform. He opposed both King CAROL and the IRON GUARD dictatorship. When the communists came into power (1946) he was denounced as a reactionary, tried for treason, and (1947) imprisoned for life.

Mannerheim, Baron Carl Gustav Emil (1867-1951) Finnish field marshal. He rose to the rank of general in the Russian army. From January to May, 1918, he led the victorious anti-revolutionary Finnish armies. In 1919 he was regent of Finland. He emerged from retirement in 1931 to head Finland's defense council. He commanded Finland's troops in the war against Russia (1939-40; 1941-44). In 1944 he became president of Finland, but resigned in 1946. The Mannerheim Line, a line of defenses against Russia, was planned by him. It was captured and destroyed (1940) by the Russians.

Mao Tse-Tung (1893-) Chinese revolutionary and statesman. Helped found the communist party in China in 1921. Led the communist army against the Japanese invasion of China (1937-1945). He is head of the Central Committee of the Chinese Communist Party, and Chairman of the communist People's Republic of China (1949-). He is considered an important communist theoretician.

"March on Rome" (1922) At the Fascist National Congress in Naples in Oct. 1922, Mussolini delivered a threatening speech in which he specifically invoked force as a justifiable method of getting control of the government of Italy. Following this speech he entrained for Milan. His followers began to concentrate on Rome. Although the army might have scattered them, King Victor Emmanuel refused to invoke martial law. Instead he asked Premier Facta to resign. On Oct. 29, the king asked Mussolini to form a cabinet. On Oct. 30, the new cabinet predominantly composed of fascists took office. But no Socialists were appointed to the ministry. Mussolini consolidated his position *after* he was appointed to the premiership.

Marne, Second Battle of the A part of the final German offensive which was met by a victorious allied counteroffensive on the Marne River in France in July, 1918. Two hundred and seventy-five thousand American troops supported the French in stemming the German advance, achieving brilliant successes.

Marshall, George Catlett (1880-) American soldier and statesman. Army General during World War II. Secretary of State (1947-49). Created the European Recovery Program (the Marshall Plan) in 1947. Secretary of Defense (1950-51). Directed general strategy for the United Nations forces in Korea.

Marshall Plan, The In an address delivered at Harvard University in June, 1947, General Marshall (at that time Secretary of State) proposed a plan of economic aid for Europe. At a conference held in Paris the following July, 22 nations, including the USSR, discussed Marshall's proposals. Despite the active opposition of the Soviets, the conference accepted Marshall's proposals and appointed a Committee on European Economic Cooperation (CEEC). This Committee prepared a balance sheet, estimating Europe's needs for the next four years. Congress created an Economic Cooperation Administration (ECA) to administer the program. The nations participating formed an Organization for European Economic Cooperation (OEEC). During more than four years of existence, the Marshall Plan countries received about 12 billion dollars in aid from the United States. Great Britain, France, Belgium, Luxemburg, Holland, Italy, and Western Germany were the largest beneficiaries. The plan succeeded in promoting economic recovery. In 1952, the overall industrial index was 40% higher than in 1938, and the agricultural index 9% higher.

Masaryk, Jan Foreign Minister of Czechoslovakia and a proven friend of the United States. Shortly after the Communist party victory in the election of 1946 which made Clement Gottwald Communist premier of the Czechs, Masaryk suffered a violent death which was officially described at the time as suicide. Since then the suspicion has persisted that he was murdered by the Communists.

Mascicki, Ignacz (1867-1946) President of Poland (1926-39). Chemist in Switzerland (1897), teacher in a technical high school in Lvov (1912-26).

Marxism The economic and historical theories of the German economist Karl Marx (1818-1883). DIALECTICAL MATERIALISM, the core of Marx's system, is considered the basic thought of modern socialist and communist political parties.

Mau Mau An African revolutionary organization in Kenya, attempting the overthrow of British authority.

McMahon Letters (1915-1916)   A series of notes between the High Commissioner for Egypt (Henry McMahon) and the Sheriff of Mecca (Emir Hussein). A promise of independence for the Arabian parts of the Near East was given because of Arab help against the Turks in World War I. The British later claimed that this did not include Palestine. *See* BALFOUR DECLARATION.

Mendès-France, Pierre (1907-)   French statesman. Prime Minister of France (1954-55).

Mensheviks   That part of the Russian Socialist party, prior to the 1917 revolution, which was opposed to the extreme doctrines of the Bolsheviks.

Metaxas, John (1871-1941)   Greek general and statesman. Chief of staff (1915-17), but exiled as pro-German when Greece joined the Allies. He returned from exile (1920), led a counter-revolution, and was again exiled (1923-24). He was a royalist. After the king was restored (1935), he became premier (1936). He was later (1936) named dictator and (1938) dictator for life. He was directing Greek resistance to the Italian invasion when he died.

Meuse-Argonne, Battle of the   An American offensive between September 26th and November 11, 1918. It was the last general push, designed by Marshal Foch to destroy the German army and end the war. Commanded by General PERSHING, the attack was launched in the Argonne along the Meuse River in France. It was aimed at Sedan, 35 miles Northwest. Nine United States divisions, supported by artillery, tanks, and aircraft, attacked, driving the Germans from Montfaucon on September 27. A renewed attack on October 14th resulted in the capture of Romagne, followed by the destruction of the German center on November 2nd and the capture of Buzancy. With the negotiation of the armistice on November 11th, the American pursuit had reached Sedan, cutting all German communications. This offensive was the greatest battle involving American troops in World War I. Assisted on the flanks by British and French advances, more than 1,000,000 troops, operating over the seven week period, defeated 62 German divisions. They captured 26,000 enemy troops and 4,000 pieces of artillery and machine guns. American casualties aggregated 117,000 dead and wounded.

Midway Islands, Battle of In a three day battle between June 4-6, 1942 United States land and carrier-based planes decisively repulsed a heavy Japanese naval and air assault. Japanese casualties included loss of four large carriers, two heavy cruisers, and three destroyers and damage to three battleships, four cruisers, and four transports. The Japanese lost 275 planes. American losses included one carrier, one destroyer, and 150 planes. The United States fleet was commanded by Admirals Spruance and Fletcher.

Mindszenty, Joseph (1892-) Hungarian prelate. As bishop of Veszprem during World War II, he maintained such a strong anti-German attitude that he was imprisoned. In 1945, he was made archbishop of Esztergom and primate of Hungary. He was made cardinal in 1946. In 1948 he was arrested on the charge of treason by the Communist government, which he strongly opposed. After a sensational mock trial, during which he pleaded guilty to most of the charges, he was sentenced to life imprisonment. He was released during the recent Hungarian revolt (1956) and at present is living in the American Embassy.

Mollet, Guy (1905-) French statesman. Prime Minister of France (1956-57).

Molotov, Vyacheslav Mikhailovich (1890-) Russian statesman. A communist from his early youth, he changed his name from Skriabin to Molotov to escape the imperial police. After the Bolshevist Revolution, he rose rapidly in the ranks of the party. He was Chairman of the Council of the Peoples' Commissars (that is, premier of the USSR) from 1930 to 1941, when the position was taken over by Stalin. Molotov then became vice chairman. In May, 1939, he succeeded Litvinov as commissar of foreign affairs (later changed to foreign minister), a post which he held until 1949. During this period he had charge of some of the most fateful negotiations in recent Russian history: the non-aggression pact with Nazi Germany (1939), creation of the UN (1945), the various war-time conferences, etc. He has been downgraded since the death of Stalin. He was renamed Foreign Minister in 1953 and was removed from office in 1956, and given the unimportant position of Minister of State Control. He was removed from the office of Foreign Minister in 1956.

Montevideo Conference   The seventh Pan-American Conference at Montevideo, Uruguay on December 3, 1933. Specifying the "GOOD NEIGHBOR" POLICY Secretary of State Hull declared that the United States was opposed to armed intervention in inter-American affairs. In June, 1934 the United States Senate ratified the Montevideo convention which declared that "no state had the right to interfere in the external or internal affairs of another."

Montgomery, Bernard Law, 1st Viscount Montgomery of Alamein (1887-)   British field marshal. He entered the army in 1908 and rose in rank through long service. In the Second World War he commanded the 3rd Division in France until the evacuation at Dunkirk. In 1942 he was sent to Egypt, where at El Alamein he decisively defeated the Germans under Rommel, one of the turning points of the war. He led his victorious 8th Army across northern Africa in pursuit of the Germans. He led the Anglo-American invasion of Sicily and Italy. In the Allied invasion of Normandy (1944) he was commander of all ground forces until August, when he was made commander of the 21st Army Group. He headed the British occupation of Germany (1945-46). He was made field marshal (1944) and viscount (1946). He was chief of the imperial general staff (1946-48) when he was made commander-in-chief of the permanent defense of Britain, France, Belgium, Holland, and Luxemburg.

Montreux Convention (1936) This international pact re-established Turkey's right to militarize and fortify the Dardanelles. No warring powers can send their ships through the straits if Turkey is neutral. In peacetime, all commercial craft have the right of passage.

Morocco, Independence of Formerly a French protectorate, Morocco became an independent state on March 2, 1956. Later Tangiers of the Spanish protectorate of Morocco became independent and was fused with independent Morocco (May 1956). It was the 18th of May 1956 that saw the complete independence of all of Morocco.

Morrow, Dwight (1873-1931) Diplomat. Appointed by President COOLIDGE in Sept., 1927 U.S. Ambassador to Mexico. His conciliatory efforts improved troubled relations with the Mexican government arising out of Mexican land and petroleum laws restricting alien corporations and alien land ownership in Mexico. Mexican Supreme Court rulings subsequently lifted these restrictions.

Moscow Conference A meeting in 1943 of the foreign ministers of the United States, Great Britain, and the Soviet Union. The declaration of the conference contained a recognition of the need of a post-war world organization for the maintenance of international peace and security. It also recognized Austria as a defeated nation which, after the war, would be treated like all the victims of German aggression.

Moslem Brotherhood A fanatic Moslem sect that supports its ideas through the instrument of assassination and political intrigue. It has been particularly powerful in Egypt. President NASSER dissolved the Brotherhood in Egypt because of an attempt on his life (1954).

Moslem League A Pakistani political party. It formed the government in Pakistan from 1947 to 1954. It was led by Mohammed Ali Jinnah, who died in 1948.

Mountbatten, Louis Francis Albert Victor Nicholas, 1st Earl Mountbatten of Burma (1900-) British admiral and statesman. His mother was the grand-daughter of Queen Victoria. He served as midshipman during the First World War. In the Second World War he was in the destroyer service, director (1942-43) of combined operations, head of the Southeast Asia Command (1943-45). He was the last viceroy of India (1947). As governor-general of the dominion of India (1947-48) he relinquished British power to native rule (June, 1948).

Mudros, Armistice of (Oct. 30, 1918) This agreement between Turkey and the Allies took Turkey out of World War I. The Turks were forced to open the Straits, repatriate Allied prisoners, demobilize their armies, sever relations with the Central Powers, and permit Allied troops to cross Turkish territory.

Munich Conference and Agreement (The Munich Pact— Sept. 29, 1938) A critical state of affairs between Germany and Czechoslovakia developed during 1938. After the annexation of Austria, the situation of Czechoslovakia became precarious. Konrad Henlein and his Sudeten Germans kept up continual agitation. On Sept. 12, at Nuremberg, Hitler demanded that the Sudeten Germans be given the right of self-determination. This address was a signal for widespread disorders in the Sudetenland. On Sept. 15, Neville Chamberlain flew to Berchtesgaden to confer with Hitler, who bluntly stated his demand for annexation of the German areas on the basis of self-determination. Hitler threatened war if this demand were denied. England and France now pursuaded Czechoslovakia to agree to the demand. Chamberlain now visited Hitler in Godesberg (Sept. 22-23), where Hitler increased his demands, calling for the surrender of predominantly German lands at once. There followed (Sept. 24-29) a period of acute international crisis. Hitler finally agreed to one more conference, after being strongly urged to do so by Mussolini and President F. D. Roosevelt. At Munich (Sept. 29), Hitler, Ribbentrop, Mussolini, Ciano, Chamberlain, and Daladier (Premier of France), arrived at the following decisions: Evacuation of all areas of Czechoslovakia which were German between Oct. 1 and Oct. 10. England and France undertook to guarantee the new frontiers of Czechoslovakia against aggression. When the Polish and Hungarian minority questions were solved, Germany and Italy would give a like guarantee. On Sept. 30, the Czech government signed the agreement.

Mussolini, Benito (1883-1945) Italian statesman. Born in Dovia, Forli. After self-imposed exile in Switzerland, he returned to Italy and became editor of the socialist paper *Avanti*. During World War I he broke with Socialism and advocated entering the war on the side of the Allies. After serving in the war, he founded *Il Popolo d'Italia* and organized the Fascist Party. In 1922, his black-shirted followers marched on Rome, and Mussolini was made Premier of Italy. He quickly consolidated his position to that of dictator (Il Duce). He formed a concordat with the Vatican (1929). (See LATERAN ACCORD.) Later he joined with Hitler to create the Axis. He helped Franco in Spain (1936-39). He conquered Ethiopia (1936) and Albania (1939). He entered the Second World War on the side of Germany at a favorable moment (1940). But in 1943, he was compelled to resign. He was arrested, but was rescued by German paratroopers. On Aug. 28, 1945, he was captured by Italian partisans at Dongo on Lake Como, and, after a drum-head court trial, was shot. His corpse, hanging head down, was exposed to ridicule in Milan.

Mustafa Kemal Ataturk (1880-1938)   Turkish general and statesman. Born in Salonika. General in the First World War. He was the chief founder and director of the Turkish Republic, and was its first president (1923-35). He set up a program of "Westernization." Within 15 years his rule changed Turkey profoundly, even in the minutest aspects of its life.

Mutual Security Act   Passed by Congress in October, 1951 as a replacement for the expiring Economic Cooperation Administration. The law authorized $7,483,000,-000 for foreign aid in the form of military and economic supplies. On October 31st Congress appropriated $8,117,000 for the first year's operation of the agency, to begin on January 1, 1952. In March, 1952 President TRUMAN requested an additional appropriation of $7,900,000,000, 90 percent of which was to be applied to military expenditures. The Act is administered by a Mutual Security Administration.

Mutual Security Program   The Mutual Security Program is a plan devised by the United States to assist friendly nations and to strengthen the defenses of the free world. It is divided into three channels: military aid, economic aid, and Point Four. There is a Director for

Mutual Security who coordinates the entire program. Military aid is administered by the Department of Defense. Point Four is administered by the State Department.

N

Nasser, Gamal Abdel (1918-) Egyptian soldier and statesman. As the head of the Free Officer's Movement he led the 1952 revolt against the Egyptian monarchy. Prime Minister of Egypt in 1954. In 1954 he negotiated the withdrawal of British forces from the Suez Canal area. He became President in a one party election in 1956. Immediately following the election he nationalized the Suez Canal Co., supposedly to gain funds for his Aswan Dam project. The British and French attempted to retake the Canal. International sympathy supported Nasser's claim, forcing the Anglo-French forces to withdraw. He became President of the UNITED ARAB REPUBLIC, a federation of Egypt, Syria and Yemen in 1958.

National Assembly of France The present law-making body of the Fourth Republic. There have been many National Assemblies in French history. For the famous National Assembly of the Revolution, see French Revolution.

Nationalism The sentiment of patriotism directed towards a national state. In the colonial period national feeling was weak, individual patriotism being absorbed with local and colonial affairs. Although a strong nationalist group emerged at the Constitutional Convention under the leadership of Hamilton, Wilson, Washington, and Jay, powerful States Rights feelings predominated in the first decades of the nation's history. The War of 1812 was the strongest stimulant to nationalism up to that time. States Rights sentiment, as manifested by the defunct Federalist Party in the resolutions of the Hartford Convention, was swallowed up by the resurgent nationalist feeling reflected in the "Era of Good Feeling." Between 1816 and the rise of the Whigs in the late 1830's virtually all aspects of American growth expressed the nationalist trend. Manifestations of this included the first protective tariff of 1816, the renewal of the charter of the Bank of the United States, internal improvements, Clay's "American System," John Marshall's decisions, and the development of a school of native literary figures dealing with purely domestic themes. Among these were James Fenimore Cooper, Washington Irving, Henry W. Longfellow, and Nathaniel Hawthorne.

"National Ministry" of Britain (1931-1945) Organized on Aug. 24, 1931, it contained members of the three major parties of Britain. Its purpose was to solve the economic distress of the country and later the critical international situation which followed it immediately on a coalition, rather than on a partisan, basis. Shortly after the formation of this ministry, the Labor Party expelled MacDonald, Snowden, and Thomas for "desertion." The National Ministry was headed by MacDonald (1931-35), Baldwin (1935-37), Neville Chamberlain (1937-40), and Churchill (1940-45). It was supplanted in 1945 by the Labor Ministry.

National Socialist German Workers' Party (Nazi) A German party which Hiter joined in 1919 and which he later led. This party envisioned a "Third Reich," a Greater Germany wherein all should be united because of their pure German blood. The party called for the repudiation of the Treaties of Versailles and

St. Germain, refutation of war guilt, revision of all reparations, reacquisition of colonies, expulsion of all persons not of German blood, governmental assurance of employment, abolition of unearned income and high interest, nationalization of trusts and department stores, and parity with other great powers in armaments. Although this program was later much modified, the catchwords of the movement remained anti-Semitism and anti-Bolshevism. The chief pillar of the Hitler movement was the white-collar section of the middle class. Army officers, anti-Semites, professors, small business men, farmers, and college students also gave the party much support. Many large industrialists, notably Fritz Thyssen, were Hitlerites. Labor and some of the strong Catholic districts gave Hitler small support. The party eventually secured control of the government (1933) and destroyed the Weimar Republic.

Nazi-Soviet Pact (Aug. 23, 1939)   Acting through Foreign Ministers von Ribbentrop and Molotov, Germany and the Soviet Union signed a non-aggression pact. This agreement, effective at once and for 10 years, provided that neither state would wage war upon the other. Neither would support a third power in case it attacked either signatory. They would consult each other in the future on all matters of common interest. They would refrain from associating with any grouping of powers aimed at the other. By a secret agreement (first made public in 1948), they divided eastern Europe into German and Soviet spheres. This pact freed Hitler to attack western Europe. It was a monumental reversal of Hitler's anti-Russian policy.

Nehru, Jawaharlal (1889-)   Indian nationalist leader and statesman. Studied in England for the Bar, (1912). Joined Gandhi's non-violence movement in India. He was imprisoned many times by the British authorities for his independence activities. Prime Minister of the Dominion of India (1947-). He is the Leader of the INDIAN NATIONAL CONGRESS. He advocates a neutralist line for India in the "COLD WAR."

Neo-Destour A Tunisian political party. It is headed by HABIB BOURGUIBA.

NEP (New Economic Policy) Soviet Union—1921-1927. A strategic retreat from socialism towards capitalism made necessary by the chaotic conditions following the inception of the Revolution and the Civil War. It substituted taxation for levy in kind. It permitted peasants to sell surplus food directly to consumers and permitted small-scale industry. Limited foreign investment was allowed. Forced labor was abolished.

Neutrality Under international law the status of governments which take no part in an existing war. Such governments refrain from granting direct aid to the belligerents. Neutral nations are enjoined to deal with the belligerents impartially in the furnishing of indirect aid.

Neutrality Acts A series of laws passed in 1935, 1936, 1937, and 1939 for the purpose of maintaining the NEUTRALITY of the United States in various European and Far Eastern Wars. The Act of 1935 authorized the President to embargo the sale of arms, munitions, and war materials to belligerents upon his finding that a state of war existed. The act of 1936 added loans to the forbidden list. The Act of 1937 conferred discretionary power on the President to prohibit the export on American ships of non-military materials, and included the so-called "cash-and-carry" provisions, to expire on May 1, 1939. It also provided for government licensing and control of the munitions industry in war and peace, and prohibited the arming of American ships trading with belligerent nations. The Act of 1939 was passed after the outbreak of World War II, and codified and revised all previous neutrality legislation, whose effect was to prevent Great Britain and France from purchasing arms and munitions in the United States. The Act was thus a departure from strict neutrality, performing actually as a diplomatic instrument to aid these two nations and their allies. It provided that the President could put it into effect by proclamation and omit the embargo features of the earlier statutes, although it forbade American ships to carry arms, ammunition, or implements of war. It forbade the arming of American merchant ships and their trade with belligerent ports in Europe and North Africa. The President was empowered to proclaim combat zones and forbid American ships to enter them. Goods could be shipped to European belligerent ports only on foreign ships and upon payment in the United States. This is the famous "cash-and-carry" clause. Such goods could be carried on American ships to all other places.

Ngo Dinh Diem (1901-)   Vietnamese statesman. Premier of South Vietnam (1954). President of South Vietnam (1955-).

Nicholas II (1868-1918)   Czar of Russia (1894-1917). Initiated the Hague Peace Conferences (1899, 1907). Completed the Trans-Siberian railway. Waged a losing war against Japan (1904-05). Compelled to grant a constitution (1905). Joined the Allies in World War I (1914). Compelled to abdicate (Mar. 15, 1917) because of failure of his domestic and foreign policies. Executed with his whole family by the Bolsheviks at Ekaterinburg (July, 1918).

Nine-Power Agreement on Germany (1954)   This agreement incorporated German troops within the Western European Union, overcoming French objections. The conference had been held in London, England.

Nine-Power Pact One of the treaties produced by the WASHINGTON NAVAL CONFERENCE of 1921-22.

Nkrumah, Kwame (1909-) Prime Minister of the Gold Coast colony 1951-1957. Prime Minister of Ghana (1957-).

NKVD (People's Commissariat of Internal Affairs) A secret police organization of the USSR which on July 10, 1934 replaced the OGPU (United Dept. of Political Police).

North African Invasion The first United States offensive in the European theater of operations in World War II. Commanded by General EISENHOWER, a combined army of 150,000 American and 140,000 British troops landed on the French North African coast on November 7-8, 1942. After a brief French resistance at Oran, Algiers, and Casablanca, the French under Admiral Darlan capitulated. The landing was made from a huge fleet of 500 transports guarded by 350 American and British warships. The landing points were Algiers, Casablanca, Fedhala, Oran, and Port Lyautey. The greatest casualties occurred at Casablanca and Oran. At Darlan's urging, French West Africa went over to the Allies. The Anglo-American army, assisted by Free French troops, continued the fight eastward toward Tunisia. Meanwhile, the British Eighth Army, under General Sir Bernard L. Montgomery, was pursuing the Italian and German forces westward from El Alamein. The victory occurred on May 12, 1943 when General Von Arnim surrendered his 250,000 troops. Axis casualties totalled 340,000 including 267,000 prisoners. The Germans and Italians lost 31 warships, 1696 planes, and 500,000 tons of shipping. The Allied Powers lost 657 planes.

North Atlantic Pact, The In June, 1948, the United States Senate adopted the Vandenberg Resolution, favoring membership of the United States in a regional scheme for defense, as allowed under the UN Charter. Conversations were then conducted with Canada, the states which signed the BRUSSELS PACT (q.v.), Portugal, Italy, Iceland, Norway, and Denmark. Sweden was invited to participate in the discussions but refused, because of its proximity to the Soviet Union. After discussions, these countries signed a mutual-defense agreement in Washington (April 4, 1949). The treaty was ratified by the Senate in July, 1949. (See: NATO.)

North Atlantic Treaty Organization (NATO) As a result of conferences among the leaders of the Atlantic Community (U.S., Canada, Iceland, Norway, Denmark, Holland, Great Britain, Belgium, Luxemburg, France, Portugal, and Italy), a permanent North Atlantic Treaty Organization was formed in 1949. The original membership was later increased to 14 by the admission of Greece and Turkey in 1951, and to 15 with the admission of West Germany in 1955. NATO consists of two divisions—civilian and military. The civilian branch consists of a Council of Foreign Ministers, who meet frequently to determine policy. It is under the charge of a Secretary-General. The military branch is under the command of the Supreme Allied Commander in Europe (SACEUR). The first Secretary-General was Lord Ismay; the first SACEUR was General Eisenhower.

North Korea, Creation of The Soviet-occupied part of Korea became the People's Democratic Republic of Korea in 1948. Its government is dominated by the communist party. It claims to represent all of Korea in opposition to the claims of the Syngman Rhee government in the south.

Nuremberg Laws (1935) A law passed in Germany in 1935 for the "protection of German Blood and

Honor." The Jews were defined as a race, and almost all civil rights were taken away from them. They were prohibited from: voting, holding civil service positions, intermarriage with Germans, displaying the German flag, and citizenship. Two Jewish grandparents was the minimum condition for being considered a Jew. These laws were strictly enforced in Germany until 1945.

Nuremberg Trials According to agreements reached at Yalta (1945) and Potsdam (1945), various Nazi leaders were tried before a Four-Power International Military Tribunal. This court convened in Nuremberg in November, 1945. Twenty-two top Nazis were brought before this court. They were charged with being war criminals because (1) they had participated in a conspiracy to commit crimes against the peace and against humanity; (2) they had planned and executed a war of aggression; (3) they had violated the rules of warfare by mistreatment of civilians and prisoners of war; (4) they had murdered and enslaved people because of race, religion, or political belief. On Oct. 1946, the court condemned 12 to death by hanging; seven were sent to prison for terms of 10 years to life; and three were set free. Separate trials of lesser Nazis were held from time to time. All told, 1539 Nazis were convicted of various crimes; of these, 444 were sentenced to death.

Nye Committee Set up in 1934 under the chairmanship of Senator Gerald P. Nye of North Dakota to investigate the activities of munitions makers prior to and during World War I. The Committee reported finding that munitions makers had realized scandalously high profits, had studiously opposed disarmament and showed unmistakable sympathies toward the Allies. From this the Committee made the unwarranted conclusion that United States policy in entering the war had been dictated by "merchants of death" and bankers. Immediate results of these disclosures were the Johnson Debt Default Act of 1934 and the Neutrality legislation of 1935-7.

O

Occupation of Germany   According to the first statement in the Declaration of the YALTA CONFERENCE, the United States, Great Britain, and the Soviet Union agreed that a central Allied Control Council, consisting of the supreme commanders of the three powers with headquarters in Berlin, be established to govern a defeated Germany. The three powers were each to occupy a separate zone of Germany, their work to be coordinated by the Control Council. France was to be invited to take over a zone of occupation and to participate as a fourth member of the Control Council. In 1945 Germany was divided into four national occupation zones, each headed by a military governor, assisted by supervisory and operating staffs. To the United States was given the territory bounded on the east by the Russian zone and Czechoslovakia, on the north by the British zone, on the west by the French zone, and on the south by Austria. The area of Greater Berlin was established, to be administered by the Inter-Allied governing bodies, with representatives of the four powers. This area is located within but is not part of the Soviet zone. Problems of government have consistently troubled the Control Council's work, culminating in 1948 in the virtual partition of Germany into two zones under rival political and economic control. After repeated vetoes the Soviet delegation left the Control Council on March 20, 1948, and on May 31 the United States, Britain, France, and the Benelux nations agreed to establish a German state comprising the three Western zones. Simultaneously the western powers introduced a new German currency. The immediate Soviet response was the declaration of a blockade on all ground communications between the Western zones and Berlin. After a year of the blockade and allied air-lift an agreement was reached by which the Soviet government agreed to remove the blockade. On September 21, 1949 the German Federal Republic came into existence when the Control Council turned over to it the administration of the United States, British, and French zones of occupation. The United States and other Western nations ended the state of war in 1951, but the U.S.S.R. did not do so until early 1955 after the allied powers had forwarded plans to grant complete sovereignty to West Germany, which was done in May, 1955. (See BONN REPUBLIC.)

Occupation Statute The document drafted by the Allied High Commission in Germany on April 8, 1949 defining the terms for the merger of the United States, British, and French zones of occupation in Germany. Following the creation of the Bonn Republic in May the powers of the Commission were set down in the Occupation Statute which took effect on September 21, 1949. It was amended on March 6, 1951 by agreement among the three Western Powers, and provided for the creation of a German Foreign Affairs ministry and the progressive relaxation of Allied control of Germany.

Oder-Neisse Line A line running from the Baltic Sea along the Oder and Neisse rivers to Czechoslovakia separating the German Democratic Republic and Poland. The establishment of this boundary gave approximately one fifth of the pre-war German state to Poland. It was established in 1945. In 1950 Poland and East Germany made this boundary permanent. It is disputed by the Western powers.

OGPU (United Department of Political Police) Created in the Soviet Union in 1922 to replace the Cheka. Its original purpose was to supervise voting and administration of the country. It became a potent secret police force. It was replaced in 1934 by the NKVD (q.v.).

"Open covenants openly arrived at." The first of President Wilson's FOURTEEN POINTS. It refers to the proposal by the President that henceforth the treaties among nations should be open to the world. Wilson did not imply, by this phrase, opposition to secret negotiations but rather to secret treaties. The principle was embodied in Article 18 of the Covenant of the LEAGUE OF NATIONS which contemplated the registration and publication of treaties.

Oran, Battle of (July 3, 1940) In the terms of the armistice with France, the Nazis promised not to make use of the French navy. The British feared that this promise would be disregarded once the ships fell into German hands. The British Cabinet unanimously voted to forestall this eventuality. On July 3, the French commandant at Mers-el-Kebir, a naval base near Oran where numerous units of the French navy were at anchor, received an ultimatum from the British Vice-Admiral Somerville demanding that the French fleet give itself up to be interned or risk sinking within six hours. The French chose the latter alternative. They were attacked and most of the ships were put out of commission, although several man-

142

aged to escape to Toulon. This "battle" greatly intensified the anti-British feeling of the French.

Organization of American States   Organized in 1948. It is made up of 21 American states who use it for purposes of mediation. The Pan-American Union is contained within its structure.

Organizzazione Volontaria per la Repressione dell'Antifascismo (OVRA) (1925)   A secret-police force which was organized in Fascist Italy and made directly responsible to Mussolini. Its function was to hunt out all those who plotted against the existing government.

Orlando, Vittorio Emanuele (1860-1952)   Italian statesman. Prime minister (1917-19). He led the Italian delegation at the Paris Peace Conference (1919). He retired from political activity at the advent of Fascism. After the fall of Mussolini (1943) he briefly reentered political life.

Outlawing of Genocide   On Dec. 9, 1948, the UN General Assembly unanimously adopted a convention branding as an international crime, the mass murder or persecution of religious, national, and racial groups.

P

Pacifism, International   During the 19th century there was a remarkable growth in the movement for international peace. In 1816 an English Peace Society was founded. In 1828 a Peace Society was organized at Geneva; a second was organized at Paris in 1841.

Thereafter many more were founded. By 1914 there were 160 similar societies with large membership. International Peace Congresses met at intervals from 1843 to 1891. In the latter year, a permanent headquarters was set up in Bern. Prominent men—Alfred Nobel, Baron D'Estournelles de Constant, Count Tolstoy, for example—gave their money, time, and talents to promote world peace. During the 1920's and 1930's the peace movement reappeared with great vigor. Peace conferences, the pledge of the Students' Union of Oxford University, the peace strikes staged by American college students, and Gandhi's doctrine of non-resistance are examples of it. At the conclusion of the Second World War, the peace movement again revived.

Pakistan, Creation of the Dominion of 1947 The predominantly Moslem areas of northeast and northwest India constitute the Dominion of Pakistan. The British government transferred authority to two governments in 1947, that of India and of Pakistan. This was as a result of the separatist movement of the MOSLEM LEAGUE. The state is not continuous, being divided into East and West Pakistan, separated from each other by a thousand miles of Indian territory.

Palestine

    See: ISRAEL, CREATION OF THE STATE OF.

Panama, Declaration of Number XIV of a series of 16 resolutions adopted in 1939 at Panama City by the "Consultative Meeting of Foreign Ministers of the American Republics." This specific declaration, consisting of four parts, stated that American waters must be kept free of any hostile act by a non-American belligerent power, that the American republics would take joint action to obtain compliance with this statement, that they would consult further if necessary, and that individual or collective patrols by the members of the waters adjacent to their coast would be undertaken whenever the need arose. The meeting itself was called to deal with conditions created by the outbreak of war in Europe on Sept. 1, 1939. Thus the Declaration set up a neutrality zone of from 300 to 1,000 miles from the coasts of the U.S. and the countries of Latin America into which the warships of belligerent nations were warned not to enter.

Pan-American Union The organization of the 21 republics of North and South America which was established on April 14, 1890 by the first Pan-American Conference. Originally known as the International Union of American Republics, after 1902 as the International Bureau of American Republics it took its present name in 1910. The Union exercises the functions of an executive committee, preparing agenda for the Pan-American Conference, arranging these conferences, and undertaking to execute the conference's decisions. Its governing board is composed of the Secretary of State of the United States and the ambassadors and ministers in Washington, D.C. of the 20 Latin American republics. It is prohibited from engaging in political activities, having been created for the purpose of fostering the commercial and cultural relations of its members. Its headquarters are located in Washington, D.C.

Panay Incident The sinking by Japanese bombers on December 12, 1937 of the United States Gunboat *Panay* and three American oil supply vessels. The attack took place on the Yangtze River in China resulting in three deaths and other casualties. The incident aroused great public resentment in the United States in a period when Japanese-American relations were already strained as a result of the Japanese attack on China that year. The demand by the United States government for redress brought a formal Japanese apology, punishment for those responsible for the attack, and an indemnity of approximately $2,250,000.

Papen, Franz von (1879-) German politician. As German military attaché in Washington during World War I, he was largely responsible for directing sabotage against munitions factories, etc. After being deported from the United States (1915), he became chief of staff of the Turkish army. He entered politics in Germany as a member of the Center Party. He was chancellor (1932) and Hitler's vice-chancellor (1933-34). In the latter capacity he signed a concordat with the Vatican. Ambassador to Austria (1936-38) and to Turkey (1939-44). Captured in 1945, he was acquitted by the Nuremberg Court. Sentenced to eight years' imprisonment by a German "denazification" court, he was released (1949) by an appeals court.

Peace Moves during World War I Long before the end of the war, various attempts were made to conclude the struggle. (1) In January and February of 1916, President Wilson's intimate adviser, Col. House, visited Europe and conferred with various leaders. This visit resulted in the House Memorandum (Feb. 22, 1916), which stated that the president was ready to propose a peace conference. The terms on which the United States would mediate included the restoration of Belgium and Serbia, the cession of Alsace-Lorraine to France, the cession of Constantinople to Russia, the independence of Poland, the transfer of the Italian-speaking parts of Austria to Italy. As the Allied leaders were then optimistic of victory, this offer came to nought. (2) Dec. 12, 1916. The Central Powers notified the United States to inform the Allies that Germany and its allies were ready to negotiate peace. No specific terms were mentioned. As the Central Powers were then at the summit of their success, the Allied governments rejected this advance. (3) Dec. 18, 1916. President Wilson submitted peace suggestions to the belligerents. He called for "peace without victory." (4) Feb. 1917. When Charles became emperor of Austria following the death of Francis Joseph (1916), he tried twice to end the war. Early in 1917 he asked his brother-in-law, Prince Sixtus of Bourbon-Parma, who had served in the Belgian army, to inform President Poincaré of France of Charles' willingness to acknowledge France's just claims to Alsace-Lorraine and to agree to the complete restoration of Belgium and Serbia. In December, Foreign Minister Czernin reiterated the offer. (5) May 10, 1917. Delegates from the Socialist parties of Russia, Germany, Austria-Hungary, Bulgaria, and several neutral states convened in Stockholm to discuss methods by which workers might end the war. Since the move was interpreted in the U.K., France, Italy and the United States as German propaganda, the governments of these four countries refused to issue passports to any of their own nationals. In September the conference broke up in failure. (6) Aug. 1, 1917. Pope Benedict XV issued a plea for a "just" and "durable" peace. He called for a restoration of all occupied territories, no indemnities, freedom of the seas, international arbitration, decrease in armaments, plebiscites to decide rival territorial claims. President Wilson, as spokesman for the Allies, rejected the idea of negotiation with the Imperial German Government. Only when the German people repudiated their "irresponsible" government would the Allies discuss peace. (7) Shortly after the Bolsheviks seized power in Russia, they tried to bring about peace by publishing the texts of the Secret Treaties to which Russia had been a party. (8) Jan. 8, 1918. In an address to Congress, President Wilson enunciated his "FOURTEEN POINTS" (q.v.).

Peace Treaties at the end of World War II For treaty with Germany, see Contractual Agreement. For treaties with Italy, Hungary, Finland, Bulgaria, and

Romania, see AXIS SATELLITES, FATE OF. Also see COUNCIL OF FOREIGN MINISTERS.

Peace Treaties of 1947 A series of treaties signed on February 10, 1947 by the United States, Great Britain, France, and the Soviet Union on the one hand and Italy, Hungary, Romania, Bulgaria, and Finland on the other. Between August and October, 1946 delegates from 21 of the UNITED NATIONS met in Paris to discuss the peace treaties with the defeated Axis Powers, Germany and Japan excepted. The treaties were thereafter drafted by the COUNCIL OF FOREIGN MINISTERS in New York City in November and December, 1946. By their terms the defeated nations were required to pay reparations in the sum of $70,000,000 (Bulgaria), $300,000,000 (Romania and Hungary), and $360,000,000 (Italy). The armies of these nations were limited to small police forces of 55,000 to 185,000 men. Italy was stripped of all her African colonies, their control going to Great Britain pending ultimate United Nations disposal. Trieste was made a free territory. Small border areas were transferred from Italy to France and Yugoslavia and the Dodecanese Islands were ceded to Greece. Transylvania was ceded by Hungary to Romania and the latter also confirmed the prior cession of Bessarabia to the Soviet Union. Hungary lost additional territory to Czechoslovakia. Limits were placed upon the navies, air forces, and armed divisions of the defeated nations. All the treaties limited border fortifications and prohibited the use of torpedo boats. The free right of all nations to navigate on the Danube River was recognized. Discrimination against races and religions was forbidden. Equal trading rights to all countries were provided for and the defeated powers agreed to repay citizens of the United Nations two-thirds of the value of property lost in those countries as a result of the war. The United States did not sign the peace treaty with Finland, not having been at war with that nation.

Permanent Court of Arbitration Also known as the Hague Tribunal. Established by the first HAGUE CONFERENCE in 1899. Each of the 45 member nations of the convention might choose not more than four individuals as members of the Court. These members constituted a panel from which the nations signing an agreement to arbitrate may choose as many as they desire. Thus a special tribunal was chosen for each case. Unless specified to the contrary all tribunals met at the Hague. Administration of the Court was supervised by a permanent Counsel and a Bureau of Registry. By the opening of World War I the Hague Tribunal had decided 14 cases although the enforceability of its decisions was constantly in question.

Permanent Court of International Justice Popularly known as the World Court. The international tribunal established by Article XIV of the Covenant of the LEAGUE OF NATIONS. The functions of the court were to hear and determine international disputes and to render advisory opinions in matters referred to it by the Council or Assembly of the League. The statute of the Court was principally drawn up by Elihu Root, former Secretary of War and Secretary of State of the United States. Although the United States never became a member of the Court four prominent Americans served it as judges; John Bassett Moore, Charles Evans Hughes, Frank B. Kellogg, and Manley O. Hudson. The opposition of irreconcilable Isolationist Senators, using the argument that membership was "the backdoor to the League," prevented entry. In 1926 the Senate voted adherence to the Court with five reservations. The last and the most serious of these declared that the Court could not without the consent of the United States "entertain any request for an advisory opinion touching any dispute or question in which the United States has or claims an interest." The Court refused to accept this reservation. In 1929 an attempt was made to amend the statute of the Court to meet the objections of the United States. The Root Protocol was accepted by the other members but the Senate nevertheless voted down American entry. The final session of the League of Nations dissolved this court since the already organized United Nations had its own International Court of Justice.

Peron, Juan Domingo (1896-) Argentine statesman. Virtual dictator of Argentina 1946-1955.

Pershing, John Joseph (1860-1948) American soldier. He was the commander of the American Expeditionary Force in France in World War I. He was the first man to receive the rank of General of the Armies of the United States since George Washington.

Petrograd Soviet of Workers' and Soldiers' Deputies This Soviet played an important part in the Russian Revolution of 1917. Activities of this body precipitated events which led to the abdication of Czar Nicholas II of Russia (March 15, 1917). It issued (March 14) the famous "Order Number 1" to the army which led to the destruction of the army, since it transferred command from the officers to soviets to be chosen by each army unit.

Philippine Islands A republic established in 1946 by the McDuffie-Tydings Act of 1934. It is the northeastern part of the Malayan Archipelago, comprising all large and seven thousand smaller islands. Its population of 21,800,000 people lives in an area of 115,600 square miles, and consists of a mixture of native Filipinos, Chinese, Japanese, Americans, and others. Manila, the capital and chief port, has a population of 1,000,000. Other important cities are Cebu, Davao, and Zamboanga. The principal languages are Tagalog, Spanish and English, although 64 other languages and dialects are spoken. Roughly 90 per cent of the people are Roman Catholic, the remainder being Mohammedan, Protestant and pagan. The Archipelago was first discovered by Magellan in 1521 and claimed for Spain. It was ceded to the United States in 1898, under the terms of the Treaty of Paris. A civil-military government was established for the Islands in 1901, which was modified by the Jones Act of 1916, and the Tydings-McDuffie Act of 1934. During World War II a commonwealth government-in-exile carried on the struggle against the Japanese until the recapture of the Islands by the United States in 1944. The outstanding president of the Philippine Islands was Manuel Quezon.

"Phony War" (Oct. 1939–April, 1940) A period in World War II between the conquest of Poland and the invasion of Norway. Because no military operations were undertaken by either side, the period was called the "Phony War" or the "Sitzkrieg."

Pilsudski, Josef (1867-1935) Polish general and statesman. Born in the province of Wilno. In his youth he joined the Young Poles. He served five years in Siberia (1887-1892) for complicity in a plot on the life of Czar Alexander III. He continued his agitation for a free Poland until 1914. He then organized an army of 10,000 which fought with Austria against the Russians. He resigned (1916) and worked independently for Polish independence. He was imprisoned by the Germans (1917-18). After the collapse of the Central Powers, he returned to Warsaw. He was elected chief of state, head of the Polish army, and marshal (1920). He directed the war against Lithuanians, Ukrainians, and Bolsheviks (1919-20). He was dictator of Poland until a constitution was ratified (1921). From 1926 to his death he was virtual dictator of his country. He was premier (1926-28, 1930) and minister of war (1926-35).

Pius XI (name **Achille Ambrogio Damiane Ratti**) (1857-1939) Pope (1922-39). Born at Desio, Italy. Prefect of the Ambrosian Library, Milan (1907-12), subprefect and prefect of the Vatican Library (1912-18), sent to Poland as nuncio (1919-20), cardinal and archbishop of Milan (1921). Elected pope in 1922, succeeding Benedict XV. His outstanding achievement as pope was the concordat with the Italian government, ending the historic feud between the Church and state in Italy. This quarrel was concluded by the Lateran Treaty (Feb. 11, 1929).

Pius XII (name **Eugenio Pacelli**) (1876-1958) Pope (1939-1958). Nuncio to Bavaria (1917-20), Nuncio to Germany 1920-1929, cardinal (1929), sent on important papal missions (1934-38), papal secretary of state (1930-39). His pontificate has been characterized by unremitting opposition to communism, the enunciation of the doctrine of the Immaculate Conception.

Poincaré Raymond (1860-1934) French statesman. Born at Bar-le-Duc. Deputy (1887), senator (1903), Minister of Public Instruction (1894-95), Minister of Finance (1894, 1906), Premier (1911-13, 1922-24, 1926-29), President of the Republic (1913-20). He adopted an inflexible policy of opposition to a strong, prosperous Germany. He occupied the Ruhr (1923). His National Union ministry averted ruin in 1926. He is a controversial figure. Some regard him as a prophet who foresaw a powerful, militant Germany. Others maintain that his intransigent nationalism drove the German people into Hitler's arms.

Point Four Program A plan announced by President TRUMAN in his inaugural address on January 20, 1949 as a "bold new program for making the benefits of our scientific advances available for the improvement and growth of underdeveloped areas." In May, 1950

Congress appropriated $35,000,000 for the first year's program of technical assistance. On June 12-14, 1950, 50 nations in the UNITED NATIONS Economic and Social Council pledged to spend $20,012,500 for programs of soil conservation, irrigation, technical aid, public health, and associated purposes by December, 1951. The United States declared its policy of granting 60 percent of the amount raised by the U.N. organization. In January, 1951 President Truman recommended to Congress a $900,000,000 program in American investments in Asia, Africa, and Latin America during 1951. Simultaneously, Gordon Gray, head of the Point Four Program, promised economic aid through a modified United States farm price-support system, reduced subsidies to the maritime industry, tariff reductions, and extension of reciprocal trade agreements, all designed to free international trade. In March, 1952 President Truman requested that Congress appropriate $650,000,000 to finance Point Four aid during the fiscal year 1953. In April, Eric Johnston, chairman of the International Development Advisory Board, told a national conference on Point Four problems that the United States was operating technical assistance programs in 33 countries around the globe.

Poland, Fifth Partition of (Sept. 28, 1939) Two weeks after the Nazi invasion of Poland, Russian troops poured into east Poland. President Moscicki, Foreign Minister Beck, and Marshal Smigly-Rydz then fled to Romania, where they were interned. On Sept. 28, von Ribbentrop and Molotov signed a new German-Soviet treaty by which Poland was partitioned between the two conquerors. The boundary line ran through old Poland from the southwest tip of Lithuania to northeast Hungary. The USSR acquired about half the territory, but only 14 million people.

This land was incorporated into White Russia and the Ukraine. Vilnius was ceded to Lithuania. After the Nazi invasion of Russia, the USSR signed a treaty with the Polish Government-in-Exile (July 30, 1941) which declared that the German-Soviet partition of Poland was void. About 36,000 square miles of the German portion were incorporated into Germany. Teschen was ceded to Slovakia. The remaining 36,000 square miles of western Poland was called a "Gouvernement-General." Its capital was Cracow. The eventual intentions of the Germans towards this last area are not clear. Temporarily it became a depository for Poles, Jews, and 1½ million "Germans" whom the Nazis assembled from the Tyrol, the Baltic States, and eastern Poland.

Popular Front, French (1936-7) A French coalition, made up mainly of Radical Socialists, Socialists, and Communists. Headed by LÉON BLUM (q.v.), they denounced Fascism, urged the nationalization of industries, and denounced the "two hundred families" who allegedly ran France. Upon coming to power, the Popular Front enacted laws calling for the 40-hour week, collective bargaining, the closed shop, paid vacations, wage increases, and a form of compulsory arbitration in labor disputes. It reorganized the Bank of France and the coal industry and created a national wheat office to control the price of bread. The Popular Front disintegrated because of increasing conservative pressure and because its measures did not restore economic stability and prosperity to France.

Potsdam Conference A meeting of President TRUMAN, Prime Minister Attlee, and Premier Stalin in Potsdam, Germany in July 1945. The Declaration issued on July 26th contained the following provisions: the promise that the UNITED NATIONS would utterly devastate Japan unless she immediately surrendered, the authority and influence of the Japanese leaders who had begun the war were to be eliminated, Japan was to be occupied until a new peaceable government under complete guarantees were established, Japan was to be disarmed, war criminals were to stand trial, freedom of speech, religion, thought, and fundamental HUMAN RIGHTS including democratic principles, were to be allowed for the purpose of producing reparations in kind. The Declaration ended by the reiteration upon UNCONDITIONAL SURRENDER. The territorial provisions of the CAIRO DECLARATION were repeated in the Potsdam Declaration, and the Conference decided upon the major political and economic principles which would guide the occupation of Germany. The following day the Japanese government broadcast her refusal to accept these terms of surrender, but the dropping of the ATOMIC BOMBS ON HIROSHIMA and Nagasaki rendered it unnecessary to invade the Japanese home islands.

Provisional Government of Russia (1917)   Organized after the abdication of Czar Nicholas II (March 15, 1917), it attempted to run the country until it was overthrown by the Bolshevik Revolution of Nov. 6, 1917. It was headed by Prince George Lvov as chairman. Paul Milyukov was head of the Foreign Office. Alexander Kerensky was Minister of Justice.

Protective Tariff Law of Britain (1932)   Because of economic problems which had beset Britain since the end of the First World War the government abandoned the policy of Free Trade which had been in existence since 1850. Included in the tariff law was a new "corn-law," which guaranteed to British farmers about $1 a bushel for a specified quantity of home-grown wheat.

Purge, Soviet (1935-6; 1937-8)   A liquidation of "rightist"

groups and Trotskyites in the Soviet Union set off by
the assassination of S. M. Kirov (Dec. 1, 1934). Included in the purge were prominent leaders like
Kamenev, Zinoviev, Piatakov, Radek, Bukharin,
Rykov, and Yagoda.

Q

Quadragesimo Anno (May 15, 1931) An encyclical issued
by Pope Pius XI on the fortieth anniversary of *Rerum
Novarum* of Leo XIII. It deplored the fact that economic life had become hard and cruel. It advocated
a "just" wage and urged that workers be given some
share in the profits of industry. Unemployment was
called a "dreadful scourge." It was blamed, in part,
on "extreme freedom of competition." Communism
was denounced and socialism and Catholicism were
called incompatible.

Quebec Conference A conference between President
F. D. ROOSEVELT and Prime Minister Churchill, held
in Quebec, Canada, between August 11-24, 1943. In
the declaration issued at the conclusion of the conference, the two heads of state announced important
progress in limiting German submarine activity. They
also stated that the two powers had surveyed the
"whole field of world operations." At the second
Quebec Conference held between September 11-16,
1944, Roosevelt and Churchill announced that comprehensive plans had been drawn up for carrying on
the war in Europe and in the Pacific, and for creating
the peace.

Quisling, Vidkun (1887-1945) Norwegian Fascist leader.
Army major, League of Nations official, he had charge

of British interests in the USSR (1927-29). Defense minister of Norway (1931-33). He founded the Norwegian Nazi party in 1933. He was Hitler's puppet ruler in Norway from 1940 to 1945. In 1945 he gave himself up, was tried, and executed. His name is synonymous with traitor.

R

Raeder, Erich (1876-) German admiral. Chief of staff to Admiral Hipper in the battles of Dogger Bank (1915) and Jutland (1916). Appointed commander of the German navy (1935), he secretly rebuilt the navy in defiance of the Treaty of Versailles. In 1943 he was succeeded by Admiral Doenitz. Captured in 1945, he was sentenced to life imprisonment as a war criminal.

Rapallo, Treaty of (Nov. 12, 1920) An agreement between Italy and Yugoslavia which stated that Fiume was to be an independent state. Italy renounced claims to Dalmatia, except Zara. Istria was to be divided between the two countries with Italy receiving the greater part.

Rapallo, Treaty of (April 16, 1922) An agreement between the German Republic and the Soviet Union. Reciprocal consular and trade relations were reestablished, and all war claims were mutually cancelled. This treaty is considered to be a step forward in the restoration of normal diplomatic relations between the new Soviet Union and the remainder of Europe.

Rasputin, Grigori (1871-1916) Russian monk and court favorite. He gained ascendancy over the Czarina and was suspected of using his influence to betray Russia to the Germans. He was assassinated (Dec. 17, 1916) by a group of Russian nobles as a patriotic measure.

Recognition of the Soviet Union For a number of years after the Bolshevik Revolution no European country which fought among the Allies recognized the Soviet Union. The first one to do so was England (Feb. 1, 1924), when the Labor government was in power. Within two months, Italy, Norway, Austria, Greece, and Sweden also recognized the USSR. France extended de jure recognition Oct. 28, 1924. The United States recognized the USSR on Nov. 17, 1933.

Reichstag Fire (Feb. 27, 1933) Following a fire which partly destroyed the Reichstag building and which the Nazis blamed on the Communists, President von Hindenburg issued emergency decrees which suspended free speech and press, as well as other liberties. The Reichstag elections which followed soon after (March 5) gave the Nazis 44% of the vote and their Nationalist allies 8%. On March 23, with only small dissenting vote, both the Reichstag and the Reichsrat passed an Enabling Act, which gave the government dictatorial powers until April 1, 1937, thus firmly establishing the Nazi dictatorship.

Renner, Karl (1870-1950) Austrian statesman. A socialist deputy since 1907, he became head of the provisional government after the abdication of Emperor Charles I (Nov. 1918). After elections were held, he became the first chancellor of the Austrian Republic. He signed the Treaty of St. Germain for Austria. Out of the political spotlight after 1920, he became (April, 1945) premier and minister of foreign affairs of the provisional Austrian government and in Dec. 1945, he was elected president.

Reparations Reparations were charged the Central Powers by the Allies at the conclusion of World War I. These

158

payments were to compensate the civilian populations of the Allied Powers for war damage. A Reparations Commission was created to determine the amount of reparations. It was soon evident that only Germany could pay reparations and that some of these payments would have to be in goods. At the Spa Conference (July, 1920) the Commission determined that payments should be distributed as follows: France, 52%; British Empire, 22%; Italy, 10%; Belgium, 8%; Japan and Portugal, 1½%; the other Allies, 6½%. It also decided to charge 56 billion dollars. This amount was reduced (April 28, 1921) to 32 billion dollars (plus interest). Germany paid the first installment (250 million dollars) promptly. Then, German currency became so highly inflated that further payments could not be made. Accordingly, in January, 1923, French, Belgian, and Italian troops occupied the Ruhr district as far east as Dortmund, a move which the British opposed vigorously. The inhabitants of the Ruhr countered this act with passive resistance. Conditions in the Ruhr and elsewhere in Germany worsened rapidly. In September, 1923, Berlin announced the end of passive resistance. In 1924, the DAWES COMMISSION (q.v.) prepared a plan which solved the reparations problem for the next five years. In 1929, the YOUNG COMMISSION (q.v.) prepared a 58 year plan for the payment of reparations. Because of the financial difficulties caused by the depression, Germany was in no position to make reparations payments in 1931. President Hoover then proposed a Moratorium. Under this proposal all payments on Inter-Allied debts and German reparations were to be postponed from July 1, 1931 to June 30, 1932. On June 16, 1932, representatives of Germany, Belgium, France, Great Britain, Italy, and Japan met at Lausanne and agreed to set aside German reparations in consideration for payment of $714,600,000 by Germany for the general reconstruction of Europe.

To meet this debt the German government was to deposit with the Bank of International Settlement 5% bonds for the whole amount. It was soon learned that this agreement was contingent upon having the United States remit the remainder of the Inter-Allied debts. This the United States refused to do. The plan of the Lausanne Conference accordingly came to naught. It is estimated that Germany paid the various Allies 6½ billion dollars in reparations. In World War II, the principle of payment of reparations by Germany was determined at the Yalta Conference (Feb. 1945). At the Potsdam Conference (July-August, 1945) it was decided that half the German reparations were to be paid to the USSR, which agreed to pay Poland 15% of that half. The remainder was to be distributed among the United Nations by the United States and Britain. Russian reparations were paid by removing machinery and equipment from the Soviet Zone of Germany (see Dismantling). The Paris Peace Conference of 1946 imposed reparations payments on Bulgaria ($125,000,000), Finland ($300,-000,000), Hungary ($300,000,000), Italy ($360,000,-000), and Romania ($300,000,000). The United States, Britain, and France claimed no reparations from these five countries.

Reparations Commission   Established by the TREATY OF VERSAILLES for the purpose of setting the amount of REPARATIONS to be paid by Germany to the victorious Allied Powers. In 1921 the commission reduced the amount of reparations, tentatively set at $56,000,000,-000, to $32,000,000,000 plus payments of materials such as shipping, machinery, coal, and railroad rolling stock.

Rhee, Syngman (1875-)   Korean statesman. President of the Republic of Korea (South Korea) 1948-.

Ribbentrop, Joachim von (1893-1946)   Nazi statesman. A wine-merchant who became Hitler's adviser in foreign affairs. Ambassador to Great Britain (1936-38), foreign minister (1938-45). He was condemned to death as a war criminal by the Nuremberg Tribunal and executed. (See Nazi-Soviet Pact, his greatest achievement.)

Reynaud, Paul (1878-) French lawyer and politician. He held cabinet posts in 1930, '31, and '32. In 1938, as finance minister in the cabinet of DALADIER (q.v.), he followed an inflationary policy. He succeeded Daladier as premier (Mar. 1940), but resigned (May 18) in favor of Petain. He was arrested (1940) and held prisoner by the Germans until 1945. He re-entered politics as an advocate of free enterprise.

Riom Trials (1942) Instigated by the Nazis, the Vichy government of France brought many of the former leaders—for example, Daladier, Blum, Gamelin, Reynaud, Mandel—to trial. The Nazis wanted these men pronounced guilty of having *caused* the war. Actually, they were accused of having failed to *prepare* France for war. When it became evident that the trials were coming close to proving what neither Berlin nor Vichy wanted, they were indefinitely suspended. The accused remained under arrest. In 1943 they were transferred to German soil lest they be freed and assist in a United Nations' invasion attempt.

Rio Treaty See: Inter-American Treaty of Reciprocal Assistance.

Rivera, Primo de (1870-1930) Spanish statesman. Dictator of Spain (1923-1930).

Roman Question (1870-1929) During the Franco-Prussian War, the French garrison in Rome was withdrawn. King Victor Emmanuel now invited Pope Pius IX to make terms with the Italian government. When the pope refused, Italian troops occupied Rome (Sept. 1870). The royal government then conducted a plebiscite among the Romans in which the vote was an overwhelming majority in favor of joining the kingdom of Italy. The Italian government tried to reconcile the pope to this situation by enacting the Law of Papal Guarantees. The pope condemned this law and refused to accept the money offered by the royal government as indemnity. He regarded himself as a prisoner and forbade Italian Catholics to vote or hold office in the royal government. This "Roman Question" was finally settled by the Lateran Concordat with Italy in 1929.

Rome, Treaty of (1924)   An agreement between Italy and Yugoslavia, repudiating the TREATY OF RAPALLO (1920) (q.v.). Italy was to receive Fiume, while Yugoslavia received Porto-Baros and a 50-year lease of part of the Fiume harbor.

Rommel, Erwin (1891-1944)   German field marshal. An early member of the Nazi Party, he served as Hitler's bodyguard and rose high in the SS. He was made a general in the army after the Polish campaign (1939). His tank corps headed the break-through into France (1940). He trained a special body of tank troops, the Afrika Korps, for desert warfare. He had great success in North Africa and was created marshal. Defeated by Montgomery at El Alamein, he was driven into Tunisia and recalled to Germany. He was in command of German Forces in France at the time of the Allied invasion of Normandy. The manner of his death is not clear. It seems that he was ordered to take poison for complicity in the plot to assassinate Hitler in July, 1944.

Roosevelt, Franklin Delano (1882-1945)   Thirty-second President of the United States. b. Hyde Park, N. Y. Distant cousin of THEODORE ROOSEVELT. Graduated, Harvard University (1904); studied at Columbia Law School (1904-07); member of law firm of Roosevelt and O'Connor (1924-33); married distant cousin,

162

Eleanor Anna Roosevelt (1905); member, New York state senate (1910-13); leader of independent Democrats; supported WILSON for the presidency; appointed by him, Assistant Secretary of the Navy (1913-21); unsuccessful candidate for Vice-President of the United States (1920); stricken with infantile paralysis; supported ALFRED E. SMITH for the presidency (1928); successful candidate for governor of New York (1929-33); supported social legislation, developed water power projects; supported regulation of Public Utilities; elected President (1932); he was the first President of the United States to be re-elected for a third term; declared a "Bank Holiday" his second day in office; responsible for the legislative reforms known as the "New Deal"; inaugurated a program of relief and public works; secured Old Age Pensions, Unemployment Insurance, Slum clearance and Housing projects, Abolition of Child Labor and better relations between management and labor; with Winston Churchill he wrote the ATLANTIC CHARTER (August 1941); granted emergency powers by Congress to determine the country's military production and civilian economy during World War II. Conferred with Churchill, Vargas, Camacho, Chiang Kai-Shek, and Stalin on war strategy and international cooperation. Died of a cerebral hemorrhage at Warm Springs, Georgia (April 12, 1945). For his contribution to the social and economic advances of the United States, he will go down in history as an outstanding American President.

Root, Elihu (1845-1937) Statesman, diplomat. b. Clinton, New York. Graduated from Hamilton College and New York University Law School (1867). Secretary of War to McKinley and Theodore Roosevelt. Secretary of State (1905-1908). Drew up Platt Amendment for government of Cuba (1901). Negotiated the Root-Takahira Open-Door Agreement with Japan in 1908. Republican senator from New York (1909-15). After 1910 he became a member of the Permanent

Court of Arbitration at the Hague. Awarded the Nobel Peace Prize for services as President of Carnegie Endowment for International Peace in 1912.

Russian Expansionism The USSR seized the initiative immediately after the end of World War II and proceeded to bring the Baltic and Slavic nations of Europe under its control. Latvia, Lithuania, and Estonia seized in 1940, were annexed outright. Native communistic groups, strongly supported by Moscow, gained control of Yugoslavia, Czechoslovakia, Romania, Poland, Bulgaria, Hungary, and Albania. The Soviets occupied eastern Germany and eastern Austria. Around these regions the USSR erected an "iron curtain." Only Yugoslavia rebelled and escaped from Russian domination. In Greece, the Communists made a strong bid for control but failed. To checkmate Soviet expansion, a policy of containment has been designed by western Europe and the United States.

Russo-Finnish War, First (Nov. 1939–Mar. 1940) In Oct. 1939, the Soviet government demanded from Finland (1) a number of islands in the Gulf of Finland; (2) surrender of part of the Karelian Isthmus; (3) an outlet at Petsamo in the north; (4) demilitarization of the Russo-Finnish frontier; (5) a 30-year lease of the port of Hangoe. In return, Finland was to receive 2134 square miles of Russian territory. When the Finns refused, war broke out. For this aggression Russia was expelled by the League of Nations (Dec. 14, 1939). England and France wanted to help Finland, but were prevented from doing so because Norway and Sweden forbade the passage of foreign troops. After heroic defense, Finland gave in and surrendered to Russia (1) all the Karelian Isthmus; (2) the city of Viipuri; (3) all the territory around Lake Ladoga; (4) most of the islands in the Gulf of Finland; (5) enough of the Rybacki Peninsula to give the USSR dominance of the port of Petsamo and the nearby nickel mines. The USSR organized these new territories into the Karelian-Finnish Republic, which became part of the Soviet Union.

Ruthenia (Carpatho-Ukraine) A province of Czechoslovakia lying between Hungary, Romania, and Poland. It was awarded to Czechoslovakia in 1919, so that Czechoslovakia might have a common frontier with Romania and thus hem in Hungary. After Munich (1939), the Hungarians seized Ruthenia. It was intended that Ruthenia be returned to Czechoslovakia in 1945. Instead, the USSR annexed it, adding it to the Ukrainian Republic.

S

St. Germain, Treaty of (Sept. 10, 1919) An agreement between Austria and the Allies at the end of World War I. This treaty recorded the break-up of the Hapsburg dominions. Austria recognized the independence of Czechoslovakia, Yugoslavia, Hungary, and Poland. Eastern Galicia, Trentino, south Tyrol, Trieste, and Istria were ceded to various countries. The Austrian army was limited to 30,000 men. Austria was required to pay reparations for 30 years. A union (ANSCHLUSS, q.v.) between Austria and Germany was prohibited without the consent of the Council of the League of Nations.

Salazar, Antonio de Oliveira (1889-) Portuguese statesman. He is dictator of Portugal, having been Prime Minister since 1932. He is head of the only party in Portugal, the União Naçional.

Salerno Beachhead in southern Italy established by British and American forces in September, 1943 after the successful invasion of Sicily. A strong German offensive almost repulsed this landing accompanied by a bitter struggle in which off-shore firing of Allied warships was a vital factor. The landing made possible the northward advance resulting in the capture of Naples and finally Rome. Italian resistance was almost completely broken and the occupation of southern Italy reopened the Mediterranean Sea to United Nations traffic.

Salonika, Armistice of (Sept. 30, 1918)   An agreement between Bulgaria and the Allies which took Bulgaria out of World War I. The Bulgarian army was demobilized and Bulgarian territory was made available for Allied operations. Following this armistice King Ferdinand abdicated (Oct. 4), and was succeeded by his son Boris.

Sanctions This term came to mean an economic boycott of a country that resorted to war contrary to its obligations to the League of Nations. Economic sanctions were authorized under Article 16 of the Covenant. The League imposed sanctions only once: against Italy when it invaded Ethiopia (Oct. 1935). Export of arms and ammunition to Italy was forbidden. However, petroleum, iron and steel, coal and coke, all essential to Italy in the conduct of the war, were not placed on the list. Imposition of sanctions against Italy was of such little effect that sanctions were abandoned by April, 1936.

San Francisco Conference (April 25, 1945)   This conference drafted the Charter for the United Nations. It was attended by delegates from fifty nations (forty-six original members and four newly admitted). The conference was in session nine weeks. The Charter was unanimously approved by the delegates. The United

States Senate ratified it in July 28, 1945, by a vote of 89 to 2. By Oct. 24, 1945, enough nations had ratified the Charter for the document to go into effect.

Santiago Conference The fifth Pan-American Congress. It was held at Santiago, Chile in 1923. Its achievements were the adoption of the Gondra Convention for international mediation by providing a discussion period in international conflict. The Conference also attempted a reorganization of the PAN-AMERICAN UNION.

Sarajevo City in the Austrian-dominated province of Bosnia where Archduke Franz Ferdinand and his wife were assassinated on June 28, 1914 while attending a military review on the Bosnian holiday. The murders were the work of three youths who belonged to a Serbian revolutionary group (the Black Hand) and who were especially trained and brought to Bosnia for this purpose (evidently with the knowledge of Serbian and Bosnian officials). This incident was the immediate cause of the Austrian ultimatum on Serbia which touched off World War I.

Saud, Abdul Aziz Ibn (1880-1953) Arab monarch. Conquered the peninsula of Arabia and created the Kingdom of Saudi Arabia. King of Saudi Arabia, 1932-1953.

Schacht, Horace Greeley Hjalmar (1887-) German financier. President of the Reichsbank (1923-30, 1933-39). Minister in Hitler's cabinet (1933-37). He instituted a complicated system of currency controls and barter trade with foreign countries which enabled Germany to secure raw materials for its rearmament program and extended German economic influence in Central Europe, the Balkans, and South America. Being accused of taking part in a plot against Hitler (1944), he was arrested and placed in a concentration camp.

He was acquitted (1946) by the Allied Court for War Criminals at Nuremberg and (1948) by a German "denazification" court.

Scheidemann, Philipp (1865-1939) German Socialist. Minister of finance and colonies in the provisional government (1918). First chancellor of the Weimar Republic (1919).

Schuman Plan In May, 1950, Foreign Minister Robert Schuman of France proposed that the coal and steel industries of France and Germany be pooled and placed under a single international agency. After a series of conferences, Belgium, the Netherlands, Luxemburg, and Italy joined with France and West Germany in a treaty which was ratified in June, 1952. Thus was created the European Coal and Steel Community. It is managed by a nine-man High Authority which has taxing power and the right to direct and finance the modernizing of plants; to set prices, wages, and working conditions; and to control production. There is a six-member Council of ministers, which represents labor and the producing interests of the participating nations. The political interests of the six nations are represented by a 78 member common assembly chosen by the national parliaments.

Schuschnigg, Kurt von Austrian statesman born in Riva, South Tyrol. A lawyer, he became minister of justice and education under Dollfuss (1932-34). Upon the death of Dollfuss, he became chancellor (1934-38). After the ANSCHLUSS (q.v.), he was a prisoner of the Germans until 1945. In 1947 he settled in the United States.

Schutzbund (Austrian) A semi-military organization formed in Austria in the 1920's among the workers to protect the socialistic gains which they had achieved.

In 1931 the Schutzbund numbered 90,000 trained armed men. (By the Treaty of St. Germain, the Austrian army was limited to 30,000.)

Schutzstaffeln (SS) Nazi party troops (elite guard). At one and the same time a private army and a police force, these Nazi troops were drawn from Baldur von Shirach's Hitler Jugend in the early days of the movement. In 1933, 52,000 men were placed under the supervision of S.S. Chief Heinrich Himmler (q.v.). By 1939, their membership had swelled to 240,000. Their mission was the protection of the Führer and the internal security of the Reich. There were, in all, 12 branches of the SS, the main body of which was the Allgemeine, organized on a military basis and consisting of all those who were not specialists. One of their duties was the staffing of the Nazi concentration camps.

Scientific Socialism This type of Socialism was originated by Karl Marx. Marx made four significant contributions: (1) He systematized existing socialistic theories. (2) He emphasized the political, as well as the economic, character of Socialism. (3) He conferred on Socialism a philosophy and a claim to be considered a science. This philosophy, often called economic determinism, contains three formulas: (a) the course of history has always been determined by economic factors; (b) present society has been evolved out of class struggles of the past; (c) present capitalistic society will inevitably change into another type of social organization. (4) He appealed, not to theorists or philanthropists, but directly to workmen themselves.

Secretariat of the UN The Secretariat is a kind of international civil service. It is made up of a staff of permanent members, drawn from all parts of the world, who carry on the day-to-day activities and the "housekeeping" of the UN. At the head is the Secretary-General. He is elected for a term of 5 years by the General Assembly on nomination by the Security Council. He is eligible for re-election. The Secretary-General has the power to ask the Security Council to act on a matter which he believes threatens international peace, and he may appear personally before the Council or take individual action to preserve the peace.

Security Council The principal organ of the UNITED NATIONS. It is, in effect, the executive agency of that organization, exercising the responsibility for maintaining international peace and security. It consists of one delegate from each of 11 nations. The permanent members comprise China, France, the Soviet Union, the United Kingdom, and the United States. Six nonpermanent members are elected for two year terms by the General Assembly. The Council is authorized to investigate disputes which threaten international peace and security. Decisions on procedural questions are made by a vote of seven members. On all other issues the Council decides by a vote of seven members, including the concurring votes of the permanent members. A party to a dispute may not vote. The chief officer of the Security Council is a president who sits for one month. The monthly rotation is done in accordance with the English alphabet. The agency sits in continuous session and has the authority to consider all situations which threaten peace. Its powers encompass diplomatic and economic sanctions against a nation guilty of breaching the peace, including the "complete or partial interruption of economic relations and of rail, sea, air, postal, telegraphic, radio, and other means of communication, and the severance of diplomatic relations." Its military measures may include demonstrations, blockade, and other operations by the military forces of members of the United Nations. Each member of the Council has one vote. As a result of the frequent vetoing of Council action by the Soviet Union the "Little Assembly" was voted into existence on November 7, 1947 for the purpose of considering questions and making recommendations for action without submitting these to the Security Council. Reporting to the Security Council are the Military Staff Committee, ATOMIC ENERGY COMMISSION, and Commission for Conventional Armaments. In 1950 the General Assembly adopted the plan of Secretary of State Acheson which provided that if effective action by the Security Council were blocked by a veto, the Assembly could be called into special session to deal with the situation and could recommend to member states collective measures to check aggression.

Sèvres, Treaty of (Aug. 10, 1920)   An agreement between the Sultan of Turkey and the Allies at the end of World War I. The kingdom of Hejaz was made independent. Syria was to become a mandate of France. Mesopotamia and Palestine were to be mandates of England. Smyrna and its hinterland were to be administered by Greece for five years, after which a plebiscite was to be held. The Dodecanese Islands and Rhodes were to be ceded to Italy. Thrace and the remaining Aegean Islands were to be ceded to Greece. Armenia was recognized as an independent country. The Straits were to be internationalized and demilitarized. Turkey retained Constantinople and Antolia. This treaty was not recognized by the Turkish nationalist government, headed by Mustafa Kemal. The Treaty of Sèvres was later replaced by the TREATY OF LAUSANNE (q.v.).

Seyss-Inquart, Arthur (1892-1946)   Austrian Nazi. In Feb. 1938, Chancellor Schuschnigg was forced by Germany to make Seyss-Inquart minister of interior and security. On March 11, Schuschnigg resigned and Seyss-Inquart became chancellor. He invited Germany to send troops into Austria to maintain order. Thus the ANSCHLUSS (q.v.) was brought about. On March 13, Seyss-Inquart proclaimed the union of Germany and Austria. He now became governor of the Ostmark, as the Germans called Austria. In 1940, he was made Nazi governor of Holland, which he ruled ruthlessly. Captured in 1945, he was tried at Nuremberg, convicted, and hanged.

Sforza, Count Carlo (1873-1952) Italian statesman. After holding high government posts, he became foreign minister (1920-21). After heading the opposition to Mussolini for several years, he went into exile (1927). In 1942 he returned to Italy, where he took an active part in politics. He was again foreign minister (1947-48).

S.H.A.E.F. The abbreviation for the Supreme Headquarters of the Allied Expeditionary Forces in World War II. Under the command of General DWIGHT D. EISENHOWER its headquarters were originally established in London. After the successful invasion of France the headquarters were transferred to Versailles. In England S.H.A.E.F. planned and organized the great task of invading Normandy.

S.H.A.P.E. Abbreviation for Supreme Headquarters, Allied Powers in Europe. The headquarters of the allied command in Europe which was established in April, 1951 by the NORTH ATLANTIC TREATY Organization to build up the military forces of its 12 member nations. In his first report to the NATO Standing Group on April 2, 1951, General Dwight D. Eisenhower, the Supreme Commander, declared that NATO troop strength in Europe had been doubled since his appointment, and three subsidiary commands had been established for northern, central, and southern Europe, each with its own air and sea arm and supply organization.

Shepilov, Dimitri Trofimovich (1905-) Soviet statesman. Soviet Foreign Minister from 1956 to 1957.

Sihanouk, Norodom (1922-) Cambodian statesman. King of Cambodia (1941-1955). Prime Minister (1955-56).

Simon, Viscount John (1873-1954) British statesman. A lawyer, he entered politics and became an M.P. in 1906. He was knighted in 1910 and became a viscount in 1940. Solicitor-general (1910-13), Attorney-general (1913-15), Home Secretary (1915-16), Foreign Secretary (1931-35), Home Secretary (1935-37), Chancellor of the Exchequer (1937-40), and Lord Chancellor (1940-45). He will be remembered for his attempt to solve the Indian question and his determined stand against appeasement.

Smuts, Jan Christian (1870-1950) Statesman. b. Cape Colony, South Africa. Educated at Cambridge University, England. Became State Attorney of South African Republic in 1898. Fought with Dutch in Boer War, and rose to rank of general. Was one of the architects in formation of Union of South Africa in 1910. He represented South Africa at the Paris Peace Conference in 1919 and became Premier of South Africa that year, serving until his defeat in 1924. He worked closely with WILSON in drawing up the plans for the League Covenant before the Paris meeting through correspondence and he was also responsible for the notion that the Central Powers should be made liable for all damages incurred in World War I and for all postwar expenses such as war pensions. In 1939 he was again made Premier of South Africa as well as Minister of External Affairs and Defense. He was an ardent supporter of the Allies in World War

II and was South Africa's delegate to the United Nations Assembly in 1945.

Snowden, Philip, Viscount (1864-1937) British statesman. He left the civil service for journalism and politics, and became a Socialist M.P. in 1906. He was chancellor of the Exchequer in the Labor and Nationalist governments (1924, 1929-31), Lord of the Privy Seal (1931-32). As a freetrader, he broke with the government in 1932. Created viscount in 1931.

Social Democratic Party, Germany In 1863, Ferdinand Lassalle wrote the *Open Letter* in which he advocated Louis Blanc's ideas of universal suffrage and national workshops. Because of the interest which the *Open Letter* evoked, a German political party, called *Social Democrat*, was founded. Side by side with this party was the German "section" of the First Internationale, headed by Liebknecht and Bebel. Both groups fused in 1875 to form the single Social Democratic Party, which was essentially Marxist in theory. It served as a model for similar groups in other countries: in Belgium, the Socialist Party (1885); in Austria, the Social Democratic Party (1888); in France, the United Socialist Party (1905); in Great Britain, the Labor Party (1906). By 1914 every civilized country had a Socialist party whose gospel was the teachings of Karl Marx.

Socialism A social philosophy, or a system of social organization, based on the principle of the public ownership of the material instruments of production and economic service. It is essentially an economic concept, rather than a political one. The extensive confusion on this point arises mainly from two sources; first, the recognition that political action will ordinarily be required to establish socialism in a society that does not possess it; and second, the realization that socialism can hardly be expected to function with smoothness and stability in anything but a democratic

174

society. Theoretically, socialism could be established in almost any type of state, and it is significant that some of the most dictatorial forms of state characterize themselves as socialistic. However, the public ownership of the instruments of production can hardly function efficiently under government despotism, and on the other hand, a society in which socialism is well established will necessarily, and almost automatically, demand and achieve a democratic form of state. Like democracy, liberty, and freedom, to which it is closely related, socialism is a matter of relativity. It can exist in widely varying degrees of comprehensiveness. To take the United States as an example, there already exist within its economic system innumerable and widely diverse socialistic enterprises, such as publicly-owned waterworks, electric light and power systems, public schools, roads, post office, transportation facilities, Army and Navy, flood control establishments and so on through an almost interminable list. There are however, many significant differences between partial socialism and complete socialism. Under partial socialism, workers, at least in theory, have the choice between public and private employment. Under complete socialism every worker, (and it is assumed that every able bodied adult will be a worker) must be in the employ of society. The distinction between socialism and capitalism is not in the character of the productive mechanism, but in the location of the ownership of Capital, Land and Business. The effect of complete socialism would be to wipe out entirely what has been called "property" or "ownership" income, and leave only "service" or "doership" income. There need necessarily be no limitations to the accumulation of consumer goods under private ownership but there would be no possibility of deriving income from the ownership of production goods, or from what

175

in socialistic terminology is called "the exploitation of labor." In its fundamental principle, socialism is practically identical with communism. It differs from communism primarily in the matter of the tempo and method of transition, and in the basis of compensation of the worker. Communism is characteristically committed to rapid, and if necessary forcible, change, while socialism is content to make its gains by gradual, piecemeal methods. Communism, in theory, holds either that all workers should be compensated alike, no matter what their economic function or contribution, or that income should be adjusted to need.

The classless state, which looms so large in socialistic discussions, is not an integral component of socialism itself, but a goal toward which the socialistic community strives, and which it hopes eventually to attain. The assumption, quite prevalent in the United States, that socialism involves the centralized ownership and administration of all economic functions has no foundation in socialistic theory. The public units which, under socialism, would conduct the economic activities are ordinarily identified in the public mind with existing political units but they need not necessarily be so, and certainly there could be as many, and diversified, types of economic divisions as the efficiency and economy of the entire system called for. There would, naturally, be a tendency towards nation-wide integration and coordination. Historically there have been many branches of socialistic theory, such as Marxian Socialism, Fabian Socialism, Guild Socialism, National Socialism, and others. The only historical example of the establishment of virtually comprehensive socialism on a large scale is furnished by the Union of Soviet Socialist Republics.

Solomon Islands Campaign   A series of air, land, and sea battles in the southwest Pacific which were fought from August to November, 1942. The Solomon Islands were taken by Japan on March 13, 1942. On August 23, 1942 a fleet commanded by Admirals Ghormley, Fletcher, Noyes, and Turner, and including an Australian cruiser squadron, launched the attack. For six weeks scattered actions continued until the climax was reached when Admiral HALSEY's command moved in. On October 11th the Japanese lost four vessels. On October 26th they lost 130 planes while the United States lost 74 planes, a carrier, and a destroyer. On November 1st the recapture of the Islands was virtually completed with the landing on Bougainville Island, although one of the most furious naval battles in history was fought on November 13th-15th. The American victory led to the encirclement and neutralization of the Japanese base on Rabaul, New Britain. The United States loss in the Battle of Savo Island was the only naval defeat in World War II.

Somme, Battle of (July 1-Nov. 18, 1916) This was a major offensive staged by the British on the Western Front during World War I. Its objectives were to try to break the German lines and to take some pressure off the French at Verdun. During this campaign the British used tanks for the first time. The Allies conquered 125 sq. mi. of territory. The furthest advance was 7 miles. The British lost 400,000 and the French 200,000. The German losses were between 400,000 and 500,000.

Southeast Asia Collective Defense Treaty Initiated by the United States and signed at Manila (1954) by representatives of U. S., Great Britain, France, Australia, New Zealand, Philippine Republic, Thailand, and Pakistan. Provided for continuous self-help and mutual aid to develop capacity to resist armed attack and subversive activities; also, technical assistance and cooperation to strengthen equal rights and self-determination of all peoples.

Spanish-American Defense Agreement (1953) This pact provided for economic aid and arms to Spain in return for American air bases in Spain.

Spanish Civil War (1936-39) The conflict began with a revolt in the army in Melillo, Spanish Morocco. The Insurgent leaders were General Francisco Franco, General Emilio Mola (subsequently killed in an airplane crash), and General José Sanjurjo (killed in an airplane crash at the very outset). On July 30, the Insurgents set up a Junta of National Defense at Burgos. The war was fought viciously on both sides. Foreigners participated on both sides. Both Germany and Italy supported the Insurgents, recognizing the government of Gen. Franco on Nov. 18, 1936. (Franco had been appointed Chief of State on Oct. 1.) The Loyalists were supported by an International Brigade of foreign volunteers and the Soviet Union. The war ended with victory for the Franco forces when Madrid and Valencia surrendered (Mar. 28, 1939). The United States recognized the new regime April 1, 1939. On April 7, Spain announced adhesion to the German-Italian-Japanese anti-comintern pact.

Spartacus movement In 1916, Liebknecht began to publish over the signature "Spartacus" letters which denounced the German war effort. Hence, his followers came to be known as Spartacists. In November, 1918, after the abdication of William II, the Spartacists began an insurrection against the social-democratic republic which had been set up. Through their newspaper, *Die Rote Fahne* (The Red Flag), and by acts of terrorism they strove to prevent the calling of a constitutional convention. In January, 1919, the "insurrection" came to a head. Had the Spartacists been resolutely led, they might have taken over the government. The movement collapsed when on Jan. 15 both Liebknecht and ROSA LUXEMBURG were arrested and killed on the way to jail.

Stakhanovism A system of piece wages, speed-up, and competition, begun in the Soviet Union in 1935 by a coal miner, Alexei Stakhanov.

Stalin, Joseph (real name **Joseph Vissarionovich Dzhugashvili**) (1879-1953) Russian communist leader. Born near Tiflis, Georgia. There is not much accurate information available about his pre-1917 days. He was for a time a student in a theological seminary. He joined the Bolsheviks (1903) and was repeatedly exiled to Siberia, but always managed to escape. After the Russian Revolution of 1917 he became a close associate of Lenin. Peoples' commissar for nationalities (1921-23). General secretary of the Central Committee of the Communist Party (1922). After the death of Lenin (1924) he became the dominant person in the USSR. He initiated the Five Year Plans, the collectivization of farms, and the purge of the 1930's. During the Second World War he was made marshal and premier of the Soviet Union. At the Yalta, Teheran, and Potsdam Conferences he showed that he was a consummate diplomat. After the end of the war, his public appearances became less frequent than usual. His remoteness stimulated public worship that was bestowed on him. On the occasion of his 70th birthday in 1949 the praise and adulation of him reached a climax. Stalin was the author of many books, some of which have been translated into English, such as *Leninism, Problems of Leninism,* etc.

Stalingrad, Battle of (Aug. 22, 1942—Feb. 2, 1943) One of the major turning points of World War II. Up to this point the Nazi offensive against the Soviet Union was successful. Following Stalingrad, the Nazis were continually on the defensive on the eastern front. The city was strategically important as a communications center on the Volga River. The battle was waged with extreme bitterness. On Sept. 1, the Russians counterattacked northeast of Stalingrad. A gigantic Russian pincers movement developed, cutting off 22 German divisions. When the entrapped Germans finally surrendered, they had been reduced to 80,000 men.

Stauffenburg, Count Claus von (1907-1944) German officer from a family of Swabian nobles who was at the beginning of World War II, first lieutenant in a German Panzer division. In 1943 he was assigned to the African campaign where he was seriously wounded losing a hand, his right eye and half of his left hand, as well as sustaining a knee injury. He formed a close circle of officers on the German General Staff, including Rommel, Beck and Canaris, who plotted the overthrow of Hitler. It was young Stauffenburg who volunteered, because of the lack of suspicion engendered by his physical handicaps, to plant the bomb which exploded in Hitler's headquarters known as "Wolfsschanze" near Rastenburg in East Prussia. Hitler escaped serious injury and in short order the conspirators were arrested, tried by the People's Court and executed in Berlin shortly thereafter. Stauffenburg was shot immediately following the attempted assassination in the courtyard of the Bendlerstrasse in Berlin.

Stimson, Henry (1867-1950) Statesman. b. New York City. Graduated from Yale and Harvard Law School (1889-90). Appointed U.S. attorney by Theodore Roosevelt (1906-10). Served with AEF in France during World War I. Governor General to the Philippines (1927-9). Secretary of State in HOOVER cabinet (1929-33). Formulated "Stimson Doctrine" of non-recognition (q.v.). Served through World War II as Roosevelt's Secretary of War (1940-45). Author of *On Active Service in Peace and War,* 1948.

Stimson Doctrine A statement by Secretary of State Henry L. Stimson, in 1932, expressing the opposition of the United States government to the conquest of Manchuria by Japan. The doctrine condemned Japanese aggression as a violation of the "Open-Door Policy," the KELLOGG- BRIAND PACT, and the NINE-POWER TREATY. It declared that the United States would not recognize any situation that had come into existence contrary to the obligations of the Pact of Paris. This policy has been adhered to by the United States since its enunciation.

Storm Troops (Sturmabteilungen; SA) Organized originally by Capt. Röhm, this semi-military organization of "Brown Shirts" was assigned to such duties as the protection of Nazi meetings and the breaking-up of radical gatherings. The SA was disbanded by the government in April, 1932, but was recreated several months later.

Stresemann, Gustav (1878-1929) German statesman. Chancellor (1923). Foreign secretary (1923-29). He followed a post-war policy of conciliation with France. He engineered the Locarno Pact and brought Germany into the League of Nations. He advocated adoption of the Dawes and Young Plans. He shared the Nobel Peace Prize with Aristide Briand (1926). He was the outstanding statesman of the Weimar Republic.

Suhrawardy, Husain Shahid (1892-) Pakistani statesman. Head of the Awami League, political party.

Sukarno, Ahmed (1901-) Indonesian revolutionary and statesman. First President of Indonesia (1945-).

Sun Yat Sen, Dr. (Sun Wen) (1866-1925) Statesman. b. in Chungshan, in Kwangtung, China. Known widely as "The father of the Chinese Republic." Attended Hawaii College in Honolulu and continued to study medicine at Queen's College in Hong Kong. He founded the revolutionary Hsing Chung society with the aim of overthrowing the Manchu dynasty. Escaping to the United States he traveled widely building up support for his cause. Later he formed a political group which was the forerunner of the powerful Kuomintang (People's party). Returning to China he became President of the new Republican government established at Nanking. He set up subsequent constitutional and provisional governments at Canton (1921). Exiled once more he turned to Russia for help. He died in Peking in March, 1925 while on a mission to organize a national convention with North China leaders. His three close disciples were Chiang Kai-Shek, military leader, Hu Han-Min, political leader, and Wang Ching-wu, diplomat. Of them he wrote, "Chiang is too ambitious, Hu too narrow minded and Wang too generous."

Sussex Pledge A promise by the German government on May 4, 1916 that Allied merchant ships would not be destroyed without warning and without saving human lives. This pledge followed the sinking of the French passenger steamer *Sussex* in the English channel by a German submarine, with the loss of two American lives. The German statement yielded to an ultimatum by President WILSON that the United States would sever diplomatic relations with that government unless it would immediately declare an abandonment of its methods of submarine warfare against passenger and freight vessels. The violation of the Sussex pledge in January 1917, contributed to American entry into the War three months later.

Syndicalism Syndicalism is a type of French trade-unionism. Syndicalists organized workers by whole industries, rather than by trades or crafts. Syndicalists tried to bring direct pressure upon the employers by "direct action"—the general strike or sabotage. They were opposed to political action or the betterment of conditions through legislative action. Thus, Syndicalists are closely akin to revolutionary Anarchists.

T

Tanaka Memorial (1927) A statement purported to have been written by Prime Minister Baron Tanaka of Japan. It described plans for a conquest of the world by Japan.

Tannenberg, Battle of (Aug. 31, 1914) A German army under Hindenburg and Ludendorff annihilated a Russian army and completely changed the course of World War I.

Teheran Conference A meeting at Teheran, Iran of President F. D. ROOSEVELT, Prime Minister CHURCHILL, and Premier STALIN between November 28th and December 1st, 1943. The Declaration issued at the conclusion of the Conference included the agreement of Iran to facilitate the transportation of supplies to the Soviet Union in the mutual war effort and the continuing effort of these nations to assist Iran with raw materials and supplies. The BIG THREE announced that they had agreed on future war plans, particularly involving the Second Front, including specifically the scope and timing of operations. Agreement was also reached on the need for an international security organization after World War II.

Third Republic, French (1870-1940) The Third French Republic was proclaimed Sept. 4, 1870. It lasted for 70 years; no other regime since 1789 lasted for more than 18 years. Weakened seriously by losses during World War I and the economic depression of the 1930's, France was an easy victim of the onrushing Nazis during the early days of World War II. An armistice with Germany was signed June 22, 1940. The Third Republic was voted out of existence July 10, 1940 by the National Assembly at Vichy.

Tito, Josip Broz (1892-) Yugoslav leader, marshal of Yugoslavia. Son of a Croatian blacksmith, he fought in the Austro-Hungarian army against the Russians in World War I. He was captured by (or surrendered to) the Russians. He fought with the Red Army during the civil war (1918-20). He returned to Croatia as a Comintern agent. From 1929 to 1934 he was jailed as a political agitator. His movements from 1934 to 1941 are obscure although it is known that he spent some time in Moscow and working for Communist causes in both France and Russia. Then he emerged as a guerrilla leader. Despite the opposition of the Yugoslav government-in-exile and Mikhailovich, he secured the backing of the United States and Great Britain, as well as Russia. In March, 1945, he organized a federated Yugoslav government. He deposed the government of King Peter II. He suppressed internal opposition by jailing Archbishop Stepinac and executing Mikhailovich. He proceeded to organize his country upon communist principles, although he did not attempt to collectivize the land. In June, 1948, he broke with the Cominform when the latter accused him of partiality to Western "imperialism." Tito has kept his position despite hostility to the USSR and all his neighbors. He has likewise refused to give up any part of his internal communist program.

Trading with the Enemy Act An American federal law of October 6, 1917 defining trade with the CENTRAL POWERS, prohibiting such trade, and providing severe penalties for violation. The act established a licensing system over imports and exports and a conservation list of non-exportable commodities. It established the War Trade Board to assure the acquisition of essential raw materials. A blacklist of all firms suspected of carrying on commercial relations with the enemy was prepared and to such companies American exporters were denied the privilege of shipping goods. The Act also established the office of the Alien Property Custodian.

Trianon, Treaty of (June 4, 1920) An agreement between Hungary and the Allies at the end of World War I. Following the collapse of the Hapsburg rule a republic headed by Count Karolyi, was established. It was overthrown (March 21, 1919) by a communist government, headed by Béla Kun. This government became involved with Hungary's neighbors. The Romanians invaded and captured Budapest (Aug. 4) after the communists had been overthrown (Aug. 1). A monarchial government, with Admiral Horthy at its head, gained control (Jan., 1920). The Romanians withdrew under Allied pressure (Dec. 10, 1919). The Horthy government accepted the Treaty of Trianon by which Hungary lost 3/4 of its territory and 2/3 of its inhabitants. Slovakia was ceded to Czechoslovakia. Austria received western Hungary. Yugoslavia received Croatia-Slavonia and part of the Banat of Temesvar. Romania received the rest of the Banat, Transylvania, and part of the Hungarian plain. Hungary agreed to pay reparations and to limit its army to 35,000 men.

Tripartite Declaration (1950) In 1950, the U.S., France and Great Britain in a declaration stated their intentions to maintain the status quo in Palestine, after the ARAB-ISRAELI WAR.

Tripartite Security Treaty A treaty of alliance negotiated by the United States, Australia, and New Zealand on September 1, 1951. It provided for peaceful settlement of disputes among the signatories, consultation among them whenever the territorial integrity, political independence, or security of any of them was threatened in the Pacific, recognition that an armed attack in the Pacific on any of them would be dangerous to the peace and safety of them all, and the establishment of a council of their foreign ministers to consider matters concerning the implementation of the Treaty.

Trotsky, Leon (real name **Lev Davidovich Bronstein**) (1879-1940) Russian communist leader. Born near Elizavetgrad. He took active part in revolutionary activities before 1914 and was exiled and imprisoned several times. After the Russian Revolution of March, 1917, he returned to Russia and became People's Commissar for foreign affairs. He negotiated the TREATY OF BREST-LITOVSK with the Germans. He became War Commissar (1918) and organized the Red Army. In 1920 he organized labor battalions to save Russian economic life. After Lenin's death he was relegated to a minor post and later banished from Russia (1929). He was hounded from country to country until (1937) he found refuge in Mexico. Here he was murdered (Aug. 21, 1940). Author of *History of the Russian Revolution*.

Trieste, Free Territory of By the peace treaty with Italy (Feb. 1947), Trieste was separated from that nation and established as a Free Territory under the control of the UN Security Council. It was demilitarized, neutralized, and internationalized. On October 5, 1954, Trieste was divided into two parts. One including the city of Trieste itself was placed under Italian administration; the other was added to Yugoslavia.

Truman, Harry S. (1884-) Thirty-third President of the United States. b. Lamar, Missouri. Served in World War I as an artillery officer; studied law; presiding judge, Jackson County Court, Missouri (1926-34); U.S. Senator (1935-45); elected Vice-President of the United States on the Democratic ticket with F. D. ROOSEVELT as President (1944); at the death of Roosevelt (April 12, 1945) he became President; conferred with Stalin, Churchill, and Attlee at POTSDAM (1945) on the future security of the world; responsible for TRUMAN DOCTRINE (March, 1947); re-elected President (1948); called his administration Fair Deal in speech in 1948 campaign; promoted NORTH AT-LANTIC TREATY (1949); and MUTUAL SECURITY PRO-GRAM (1952); vigorous supporter of South Korea when Korean War broke out.

Truman Doctrine The name given to the anti-communist principle of foreign policy enunciated by President TRUMAN in March, 1947. In a message to Congress at that time, the President declared it to be the policy of the United States that moral and financial assistance be granted to countries whose political stability was threatened by communism. He requested that Congress appropriate $400,000,000 for military and economic aid to Greece and Turkey to whom should be sent as well American military and economic advisers. This principle has remained the basic tenet of American foreign policy during the "COLD WAR," later supplemented by the principles of the MARSHALL PLAN, the NORTH ATLANTIC TREATY, the Military Arms Program, and the MUTUAL SECURITY PROGRAM.

Trusteeship Council of the UN The UN is concerned
with the welfare of 750 million colonial people living
throughout the world. To prepare them for eventual
self-government, there has been set up the trusteeship system. Under this system there are three types
of territories: (1) territories held under League of
Nations mandates granted after World War I; (2)
colonial territories taken from the Axis during and
after World War II; (3) territories voluntarily placed
under the trusteeship system by the states responsible for their administration. The Trusteeship Council is made up of eleven members. The Big Five
(United States, France, Great Britain, USSR, China)
are guaranteed membership. Other members are
chosen by the General Assembly. Each member has
one vote, and decisions are made by a simple majority. The Council makes periodic inspections of the
trust regions. It may make specific recommendations
for reforms. There is a special class of trusteeships
called *strategic areas*. These are supervised, not by
the Trusteeship Council, but by the Security Council.

Tudeh Party Radical party in Iran, under communist
control.

"Twenty-One Demands" A series of demands made by
Japan upon China in 1915. Couched as an ultimatum,
these demands gave Japan a complete protectorate
over China. Since they violated the Open-Door Policy and the Root-Takahira Agreement of 1908, Secretary of State Bryan issued a vigorous protest. The
protest declared that the United States would not
recognize any impairment of American rights, the
open-door policy, or the territorial and political sovereignty of China. Japan ignored this note and continued her move toward domination of the Far East.
It was not until the Washington Naval Conference
that the problems of Far Eastern policies were thor-
oughly negotiated.

U

Unconditional Surrender Refers to the demand by a military or political head upon an enemy during war to surrender without negotiating any terms. In American history the phrase was first used by General U. S. Grant in his attack on Fort Donelson in 1861, as the sole terms of the Confederate surrender. It was again used during World War II by President F. D. ROOSEVELT and Prime Minister Churchill in 1943 at the CASABLANCA CONFERENCE, with reference to the AXIS POWERS.

United Arab Republic, Creation of the In Feb. 1958, a union was formed, between the States of Egypt, Syria, and Yemen. The first President was GAMAL ABDEL NASSER of Egypt. The seat of the government is in Cairo. There is no geographical unity to the Republic. Egypt and Syria are separated by Israel and Jordan. Yemen is at the Southern end of the Arabian Peninsula.

United Nations A world organization established at San Francisco on June 26, 1945 for the purpose of maintaining international peace and security. The United States Senate ratified the charter on July 28, 1945. Fifty members drew up the U. N. charter to which 25 additional nations had adhered by 1956. The charter became effective on October 24, 1945 when the requisite ratifications by the five permanent members of the SECURITY COUNCIL, joined with the ratifications of other nations attained two-thirds of the original signatories. In addition to the basic objective mentioned above, other functions of the U.N. include economic and social research, scientific development, promotion of HUMAN RIGHTS economic advancement of all peoples, settlement of DISPLACED PERSONS, health, education, and general cultural activities. The principal organs of the U.N. are the Security Council, General Assembly, Secretariat, Economic and Social Council, International Court of Justice, Permanent Chiefs of Staff, and the Trusteeship Council. There are, in addition, scores of important committees and councils engaged in *ad hoc* activities. The organization has achieved notable successes in resolving international disputes. Among these have been the withdrawal of Soviet troops from Iran in 1946, the solution of the Indonesian problem in 1949, the partition and successful conclusion of the war in Israel in 1948 and 1949, and the repulsion of the North Korean invasion in 1950-52. The United Nations may not intervene in the internal affairs of member states except to apply enforcement measures which have been legally determined in accordance with the principles of the charter. Its permanent headquarters are located in the United Nations Building in New York City.

United Nations Charter The Charter of the UN is a document of 111 articles covering all phases of international organization. In addition to the main Charter, there are the charters of the many specialized agencies through which the UN accomplishes its purposes. The aims of the UN, as stated in the Charter, are (1) to maintain international peace and security by collective action; (2) to develop friendly relations among the nations; (3) to achieve international cooperation in solving economic, social, cultural or humanitarian problems and in promoting respect for human rights and fundamental freedoms; (4) to serve as a center for harmonizing the actions of nations in the attainment of these common ends. The principal organs of the UN are the General Assembly, the Security Council, the Economic and Social Council, the Trusteeship Council, the International Court of Justice, and the Secretariat. (See separate listing for discussion of each organ. See also Specialized Agencies of the UN.)

United Nations Educational, Scientific, and Cultural Organization (UNESCO) The object of UNESCO is to insure peace through international understanding. It has undertaken many projects to restore schools that were destroyed during the war; to stimulate the free interchange of ideas through travel, films, broadcasts, and publications; to reduce illiteracy; to sponsor international cultural exchanges through music, the theatre, art, and literature; and to encourage the interchange of scientists, educators, and students.

United Nations Relief and Rehabilitation Administration (UNRRA) An organization founded Nov. 9, 1943 to give aid to those regions which had been liberated from the Axis. Altogether, 52 countries participated. Of the 4 billion dollars which was spent, half was contributed by the United States. The three directors—Fiorello La Guardia, Herbert Lehman, and Gen. Lowell Rooks—were Americans. China, Czechoslovakia, Greece, Italy, Poland, the Ukraine, and Yugoslavia were the chief recipients of aid. The organization returned 7 million displaced persons to their homelands and maintained camps for one million more. The European operations ended July 30, 1947; those in China, March 31, 1949. Much of the work formerly done by UNRRA was taken over by UN organizations, such as the Food and Agricultural Organization and the International Refugee Organization.

United States-Japanese Security Treaty Negotiated in San Francisco on September 8, 1951. By its terms Japan grants to the United States the right to station land, air, and sea forces on or about her islands. These forces are designed to maintain the international peace and security of the Far East and the security of Japan against armed attack by a third party. The

United States may also, at the request of Japan, suppress internal "riots and disturbances" instigated by an outside power. Japan is forbidden to grant bases, rights, powers, or authority to any third power without the consent of the United States. The Treaty will expire when, in the opinion of the governments of the signatory powers, the UNITED NATIONS shall have arranged satisfactory methods of providing for the peace and security of the Japanese area. The Senate ratified the treaty on March 20, 1952.

United States Trusteeships The Strategic Trust Territory of the Pacific Islands, assigned to the United States by the UNITED NATIONS in 1947 as trusts. The territory consists of the Mariana Islands, Caroline Islands, and Marshall Islands. The entire group constitutes over 1,400 islands with a total land area of 830 square miles. The three groups were sold to Germany by Spain in 1899, occupied by Japan in 1914, and mandated to Japan in 1920 by the LEAGUE OF NATIONS. The assignment of the trust was approved by Congress on July 18, 1947, and its administration conferred upon the Navy Department. On July 1, 1951 they were transferred to the Department of the Interior.

Universal Declaration of the Rights of Man (1948) A declaration adopted by the United Nations General Assembly. It set down minimum social rights that should be available to all men.

U Nu (1907-) Burmese revolutionary and statesman. Prime Minister of Burma (1948-1956).

Unrestricted Submarine Warfare On January 31, 1917 the German foreign minister, Von Bernstorff, informed the United States government that, on the following day, unrestricted Submarine warfare would be resumed. He declared that German submarines would sink on sight all merchant vessels, whether armed or not, within a military zone around the

British isles and the Mediterranean Sea. The German government offered to permit passage of one passenger vessel a week, plainly marked with red and white stripes on her hull and funnels and carrying a checkered flag at each masthead. This vessel was to carry no contraband and was to travel through a narrow lane of safety to the English coast. This violation of the SUSSEX PLEDGE was followed on February 3rd by the severance of diplomatic relations between the United States and Germany.

Utopian Socialism A social development in the first half of the 19th century. It took the form of organized cooperative and semi-socialist communities established in various eastern and mid-western states. The philosophy of the movement grew out of the belief in the innate goodness of men who would voluntarily relinquish their worldly wealth to the less fortunate, and accommodate themselves to cooperative living. This reform movement was an outgrowth and part of the social upheaval of the Jacksonian movement, reflecting the reform demands of the Frontier. Among the various experiments were the German Separatists movement at Zoar, Ohio in 1817, the Oneida Community in New York organized by John Humphrey Noyes in 1848, the New Harmony establishment in Indiana founded by Robert Owen in 1825, and in 1841, the Brook Farm experiment originated by the members of the Transcendental Club of Boston including George Ripley, Charles A. Dana, and Nathaniel Hawthorne, and the Icarian movement in Texas established by Étienne Cabet in 1848. These communities were uniformly unsuccessful, their failures resulting from improper administration, the visionary views of their founders, inadequate financing, public opposition, and the physical destruction of many of them by fire and storm.

V

V-1 and V-2 V-1 and V-2 *Vergeltungswaffe*, or "vengeance weapons." These German weapons were first launched against England on June 13, 1944. V-attacks continued until the forces of the United Nations captured all the launching fields in Europe. The V-1 was a pilotless, jet-propelled bomb. About 2300 of them got through to London, where they killed or wounded 20,000 people. In Sept. 1944, the attacks of V-1's ceased. Then began the V-2 attacks. These weapons were rockets which shot through the stratosphere at supersonic speed. The Germans continued to send them against England until the spring of 1945.

Vera Cruz Incident. Refers to the arrest of United States marines in Tampico in 1914, followed by the dispatch of an American fleet and the landing of troops at Vera Cruz on April 21st. The city was bombarded and captured with the loss of 17 American dead and wounded. The order by President WILSON followed the refusal of the Mexican government to grant a 21 gun salute to the American Flag despite the fact that the Marines had been released and apologies offered.

Verdun, Battle of (Feb. 21—July 11, 1916) The Germans tried to break through the French front in World War I by striking "at the heart of France." The German troops were led by Crown Prince William. The French defense was organized by General (later Marshal) Pétain, who coined the famous phrase "They shall not pass." Later Pétain was replaced by General Nivelle. At the end of the campaign the opposing lines were in virtually the same positions as before the engagement.

194

Versailles, Peace Conference of This conference convened in Paris on Jan. 18, 1919 for the purpose of conducting peace with Germany, following the end of World War I. Seventy delegates, representing 27 of the victorious nations, gathered in Paris. Full sessions of the conference were of little importance. From the beginning, decisions were made by the Supreme Council (Big Ten), composed of Wilson, Lansing, Lloyd George, Balfour, Clemenceau, Pichon, Orlando, Sonnino, Saionji, and Makino. On March 25, the Big Ten was replaced by the Big Four (Wilson, Lloyd George, Clemenceau, and Orlando). The Japanese withdrew from deliberations of the Supreme Council after their ambitions in the Pacific were fully satisfied. The Big Four really became the Big Three when Orlando and Wilson disagreed over the Fiume question. On April 28 the Covenant of the League of Nations was presented in its final form. The authors of the covenant were Wilson, House, Cecil, Smuts, Bourgeois, and Venizelos. The conference was marked by violent controversies. Clemenceau insisted upon the cession by Germany of the left bank of the Rhine and the annexation by France of the Saar Basin. Wilson and Lloyd George opposed these demands. England and France insisted that Germany must pay all the costs of the war. Wilson objected to this proposition. The Polish claims (supported by France), the Japanese intentions toward Shantung, and the Italian claims to the Dalmatian coast also were major matters of discord. (The Italian delegates left the conference on April 23 and did not return until May 7.) All these questions were finally settled by compromise. The treaty was submitted to the German delegation on May 7. The Germans protested against the terms of the treaty as violating the armistice agreement. After an acute domestic crisis, the Germans agreed to sign. The signing of the treaty took place on June 28 (five years to the day after the assassination of Archduke Francis Ferdinand at Sarajevo) in the Hall of Mirrors in Versailles.

Versailles, Treaty of The treaty which ended World War I. It was signed in June, 1919 by 32 nations, and was submitted for German signature. It consisted of 440 articles. Among the important clauses were a statement of sole German war guilt, the demilitarization of the Rhineland, the cession of the Saar Valley coal mines to France, a limitation of the German army to 100,000 men, the abolition of the German general staff, the prohibition of German naval and military air forces, the repayment by Germany to the Allies, ton for ton, of all Allied shipping sunk during the war, the stripping from Germany of all her colonies, the imposition of an indemnity of $5,000,000,000 and of a future REPARATION bill of an indeterminate amount, and the loss of much territory in Europe. Among the latter were the cession of Alsace and Lorraine to France, the Sudetenland to Czechoslovakia, Eupen, Malmédy, and Moresnet to Belgium, the Polish Corridor to Poland, and the creation of the free city of Danzig to be administered by the League of Nations. The Covenant of the LEAGUE OF NATIONS was the first clause of the treaty. The Treaty was not ratified by the United States Senate, although it received a majority of the Senate votes on November 19, 1919, and on March 19, 1920. The Republican "irreconcilables" led by Senators Lodge, Borah, and Johnson succeeded in defeating American ratification.

Vichy Government of France By the terms of the German-French armistice (June 22, 1940) in the Second World War, France was divided into two parts by a line which ran from the Swiss border near Geneva to a point 12 miles east of Tours. The line then ran to the southwest to St. Jean Pied de Port. The Germans occupied the northern portion, which included most of the industrial regions of France, Paris, and the Channel and Atlantic coast. Unoccupied France was ruled from Vichy, where Marshal Pétain ruled as "Chief of State." A National Assembly of two houses was entrusted with the task of preparing a constitution (July 10, 1940). Being dilatory in its duty, in August, 1940, Pétain abolished the National Assembly and ruled by decree. Pierre Laval was designated as Pétain's successor. In Dec. 1940, Laval was removed from office and was succeeded by Admiral Darlan. In April, 1942, the Nazis persuaded Pétain to restore Laval to authority as "chief of government." The Vichy government took as its motto "Labor, Family, Fatherland." It enacted anti-Semitic laws, forbade labor unions and strikes, revised the inheritance laws to perpetuate the peasant basis of agriculture, regulated every phase of economic life.

Victor Emmanuel III (1869-1947) King of Italy from 1900 to 1946 (from 1944 in name only). The first World War added greatly to his kingdom. A tool of Mussolini from 1922. The Second World War stripped him of the empire of Ethiopia and the kingdom of Albania. He abdicated in 1946.

Vietnam, Independence of The Republic of Vietnam came into existence in 1945 after the end of Japanese occupation. The leader of the government was HO CHI-MINH. The new republic fought the returning French forces after negotiations with the French government had broken down. In 1954 the Geneva Agreements brought about the creation of two states. One was the communist-controlled Viet-Minh government in the north (above the 17th parallel), the other was the French-backed Vietnam government of the south.

Vishinsky, Andrei Yanuarievich (1883-1954) Russian jurist and diplomat. After studying law, he entered the

Social Democratic Party. He fought in the Bolshevik ranks through the civil wars. He was appointed state prosecutor (1923) and rector of the University of Moscow (1925). He was the prosecutor who conducted the purges of 1936-38 (see PURGE, SOVIET). After the start of the Second World War, he became a diplomat, representing his country on the Allied Mediterranean Commission and the Allied Advisory Council for Italy (1943-45) and in the Balkans, particularly in Romania. After the creation of the United Nations, he was one of the key figures there. In 1949, he replaced Molotov as foreign minister of the USSR. On the death of Stalin (1953), he was replaced by Molotov and appointed instead to be chief USSR delegate to the UN. He died suddenly in New York City in 1954.

Voice of America An international short wave radio series established as the International Broadcasting Service in the Department of State by congressional act of January 27, 1948. Its functions were to communicate with persons in occupied and hostile countries by daily broadcasts all over the world. In 1948 a new policy led to the discontinuance of the issuance of news reports in favor of more intensive and direct propaganda following protests against broadcasts to Latin America. In 1950 Congress' appropriations included $2,800,000 for the purchase and distribution of radio receivers in Communist countries and other important areas. In 1952 the Voice of America employed 1,700 people in its programs which originated in New York City, Washington, D. C., and Munich, Germany. The service operated relay stations in the United States and Europe in carrying broadcasts in 46 languages to a potential audience of 300,000,000 people in 35 countries. It transmitted 35 or more daily broadcasts. In that year the Voice of America received about 1,000 letters daily and mailed out 1,250,000 program schedules bi-monthly. It trans-

mitted from 74 short-wave radios of which 36 were
abroad. The service was established as part of the
State Department's Information and Education Exchange. In 1953 the Voice of America, with other
governmental information agencies, was removed
from the jurisdiction of the State Department and
placed under a separate United States Information
Agency responsible to the National Security Council
and the President.

W

Wake Island A group of three islets Wake, Wilkes, and
Peale, discovered by the British in 1796 and annexed
by the United States in 1898. They are located in
the Pacific Ocean, halfway between Midway and
GUAM. The group is four and one half miles long and
one and a half miles wide, with an area of 2,600
acres. Utilized solely as a military base, the Island,
formerly administered as part of Honolulu County,
Hawaii, is now under the jurisdiction of the Navy
Department. It was attacked by the Japanese at the
outbreak of World War II, and conquered by them
on December 23, 1941. The Japanese surrendered the
Island to the United States on September 4, 1945. On
October 15, 1950, it was the site of an important conference between President TRUMAN and General MAC-
ARTHUR, dealing with the Korean War.

War Crimes During World War II the first statement by
the UNITED NATIONS that War Crimes would be pun-

ished after the war was made in the Moscow Declaration on October 30, 1943. Subsequently the United Nations Commission for the Investigation of War Crimes was established to compile lists of suspected war criminals. It classified two groups of crimes: those against the nationals of a state, the trial of which was to be held by national courts or military tribunals, and those international in scope, to be tried by special international courts under military law. In August, 1945 the United States, England, France, and the Soviet Union adopted a statute for trying the principal Nazi civil and military leaders. These nations established the Nuremberg Tribunal which opened its hearings on November 20, 1945 for the trial of 21 top Nazi leaders. Associate Justice Robert H. Jackson, on leave from the United States Supreme Court, was the prosecutor. War crimes had been defined as plotting aggressive war, atrocities against civilians, genocide, slave labor, looting of occupied countries, and the maltreatment and murder of war prisoners. Voluminous evidence was introduced at the trial, and sentence of death was imposed on October 1, 1946, upon Göring, Streicher, Ribbentrop, and eight others. Seven were sentenced to imprisonment. No convictions were handed down against Nazi organizations or the German general staff. On June 3, 1945 trial was opened in Tokyo by an 11 man international tribunal against 28 Japanese indicted as war criminals. On November 12, 1948, sentence was handed down against 25, and on December 23, 1948 former Premier Tojo and six others were hanged in Tokyo after the failure of their appeal to the United States Supreme Court. During this period concurrent trials were held in German and Japanese courts which, by 1950, had tried more than 8,000 war criminals and executed 2,000 of them. The number of trials declined thereafter, and by 1952 many appeals by the convicted had resulted in reversals.

Warsaw Pact See EASTERN EUROPEAN MUTUAL ASSISTANCE TREATY

Washington Naval Conference A conference for the limitation of naval armaments which met in Washington, D.C. from November, 1921 to February, 1922. The participating nations were the United States, Great Britain, Japan, France, Italy, the Netherlands, Portugal, Belgium, and China. The results of the Conference included a series of treaties involving naval limitation, adjustment of Far Eastern problems, the status of China, and limitation of island fortifications in the Pacific. The Conference left Japan as the strongest naval and military power in the Far East. Although it preserved peace in the Pacific for a decade and relieved the United States from the exclusive support of the Open Door Policy, it provided the political and military means for future Japanese aggression. See Four Power Treaty, Five Power Treaty, and Nine Power Pact.

Wavell, Archibald Percival, first Earl of Cyrenaica and Winchester (1883-1950) British field marshal and Viceroy of India. He saw service in South Africa and on the Western Front in World War I, where he lost an eye. Later he served under Allenby in Palestine and there learned much about the strategy of desert fighting. In World War II he was made Middle East Commander. He repulsed the Italian invasion of Egypt (1940-41), but was later driven back by Rommel when many of his troops were diverted to Crete. In 1942, he became Allied Commander of the Southwest Pacific. He was Viceroy of India (1943-47), during which time he worked for Indian independence. Author of *The Palestine Campaigns* (1928), *Allenby* (1940), *The Good Soldier* (1947), etc.

Webb, Sidney James 1st Baron Passfield. (1859-1947). English economist, socialist, and statesman. Born in

London. One of the founders of the Fabian Society. Taught economics in the University of London (1912-27). Member of the royal commission on trade-union law (1903-06). With his wife Beatrice (*née* Potter) (1858-1943) he wrote on economics and sociology. Founded the *New Statesman* (1913). M.P. (1922-29). Secretary for the colonies and dominions (1929-31). Created Baron Passfield (1929). With his wife he wrote *History of Trade Unionism* (1894), *Industrial Democracy* (1897), *Decay of Capitalist Civilization* (1921), etc.

Weimar Constitution of the German Republic Adopted July 31, 1919. The head of the state was to be a president, chosen for a 7-year term. The president was to appoint a chancellor, who, in turn, chose a cabinet which could command a majority in the Reichstag. The president had the power to suspend constitutional guarantees and the Reichstag in a case of emergency. The Reichsrat, composed of delegates from the 18 states (Länder), could delay but not prevent legislation. The members of the Reichstag were elected, not as individuals, but by party lists for all Germany. Elections were held according to the Baden method of proportional representation whereby each party secured one delegate for each 60,000 votes that it polled. There was to be separation of church and state and complete religious liberty. All education was placed under the control of the state and all teachers were state officials. Provision was made for state insurance against sickness, accident, old age, and unemployment. All private property was to be used "to serve the public good." Article 25 empowered the president to dismiss the Reichstag and to order a new election within 60 days. Article 48 permitted the president, acting with the chancellor, in times of emergency to suspend the constitutional guarantees and to issue decrees with the force of law.

These two articles were used by the Nazis in 1933 to seize control of the government and destroy the Republic. This constitution continued in effect until March 23, 1933, when the Reichstag, by a vote of 441 to 94, passed an enabling act which virtually set aside the Weimar Constitution, leaving dictatorial powers in Hitler's hands.

"Welfare State"   Also called the "service state." The term applied to the wide extension of social services to the people by government. Traditionally government had supplied merely protective services in the form of military, fire, and police protection, plus minimum aid to the needy and aged. The development of technology which produced the complex industrial system in modern nations raised a host of serious problems concerned with the welfare of their people. In the United States cyclical depressions have given rise to serious unemployment. This problem had paralleled the problems of old age, illness, workmen's disability, child welfare, housing, education, recreation, and poverty. The inability of private charity, state and municipal assistance to cope with these problems has led to the development of a program of federal aid.

Welles, Sumner (1892)   Diplomat. b. New York. Graduated from Harvard, 1914. Served as Secretary to Tokyo Embassy, 1915-17. Also in Buenos Aires, 1917-1919. After further service with the State department he was appointed Ambassador to Cuba (1933) and Assistant Secretary of State (1933-37). He was Undersecretary of State from 1937 to his resignation in 1943. In 1940 he traveled to Europe as President Roosevelt's special representative to sound out heads of the belligerent states in an attempt to formulate terms of peace.

Westminster, Statute of (1931)   The British Parliament, through this act, gave the Commonwealth Dominions absolute individual sovereignty.

White Army The Russian counter-revolutionary army fighting the Bolsheviks during the period 1917-1921.

Wilhelmina (1880-) Queen of the Netherlands. She succeeded her father, William III, in 1890. Despite her great influence upon the government, she was always a strictly constitutional monarch. Her court was distinguished by its simplicity and high moral tone. She lived in exile (1940-45) in the United States, Canada, and England when the Nazis occupied her country. She abdicated in 1948, and was succeeded by her daughter Juliana.

Wilson, Woodrow (Full name **Thomas Woodrow**) (1856-1924) Twenty-eighth President of the United States. b. Staunton, Virginia. Graduated, Princeton University (1879); admitted to the bar and practiced in Georgia (1882); studied political science and jurisprudence at Johns Hopkins (Ph.D. 1886); after teaching at Bryn Mawr, Wesleyan and Princeton he was made president of the latter (1902-10); elected governor of New Jersey (1911-13); supported important reform legislation including a Corrupt Practices Act, Workingmen's Compensation, and the direct Primary; with the support of William J. Bryan, he was nominated for the presidency on the Democratic ticket and elected President of the United States (1913-21); during his administration many important Acts were passed including the Clayton Anti-Trust Act, the Federal Reserve Act, the Underwood Tariff and three amendments to the Constitution (17th, 18th, and 19th); although he attempted to keep the United States neutral during the period leading up to World War I he finally directed mobilization and led the country to victory; outlined the FOURTEEN POINTS for Peace; participated in the Peace Conference and accepted the covenant of the LEAGUE OF NATIONS; he fought a losing battle for the United States to join the League; awarded the Nobel Peace Prize (1920);

attempted to campaign throughout the country for his position but suffered a nervous collapse (Sept. 1919) and never fully recovered. Author of many books on political science and world affairs. He was an important, liberal, and honest President.

Windsor, House of (until 1917 it was called the House of Saxe-Coburg-Gotha). The present royal family of England.

	Born	*Ruled*
Edward VII	1841	1901-1910
George V	1865	1910-1936
Edward VIII	1894	1936-1936

(He abdicated. He has been known since as the Duke of Windsor.)

George VI	1895	1936-1952
Elizabeth II	1926	1952-

World Disarmament Conference A conference of 57 nations which was convened by the LEAGUE OF NATIONS at Geneva, Switzerland in February, 1932 to discuss general DISARMAMENT. The United States was one of the non-member nations which participated. It was the first world conference in history to take up the limitation of armaments of every kind. To it were submitted peace memorials signed by 8,500,000 persons in 45 countries. For almost two years the nations bickered over the terms of proposed disarmament treaties. Germany demanded the right to armed equality. The Soviet delegation proposed that disarmament be complete and reasonably prompt. The French plan suggested Collective Security agreements and an international police force. President HOOVER proposed an immediate reduction of one third in existing national armaments and the outlawing of chemical warfare, bombing planes, heavy artillery, and tanks. On May 27, 1933 the United States delegate declared that his government was willing "to consult the other States" in the event of a threat to peace. The Japanese invasion of Manchuria in 1931, the accession of the Nazis to political power in Germany in January, 1933, and the withdrawal of Germany from the Conference in October, 1933 made all disarmament proposals impossible.

World Health Organization (WHO) (1948) The WHO is concerned with raising the standards of health throughout the world. It first concentrated upon eradicating malaria and tuberculosis. Through the FAO it is trying to promote better nutritional standards throughout the world.

World War I (1914-1918) Fundamental causes: (1) Imperialism and its rivalry for markets, raw materials, etc. (2) Militarism, which made Europe an armed camp. (3) Nationalism with its irredentist movements. (4) International anarchy—the absence of any established organization which might seek to settle differences between nations and work for peace. (5) The system of alliances, which enabled each member to call for assistance from all other members whenever it was confronted with some difficulty. (See Triple Alliance. See Triple Entente.) The immediate cause was the assassination of Archduke Francis Ferdinand of Austria-Hungary at Sarajevo by a Serbian nationalist. The contestants were called THE CENTRAL POWERS (q.v.) *and* THE ALLIES (q.v.). *1914.* The German supreme commander, General Helmuth von Moltke, put into operation a revised version of the so-called Schlieffen Plan. This had been prepared by General Alfred von Schlieffen, who was chief of the general staff from 1891 to 1906. Schlieffen anticipated a war on two fronts. Believing that Germany could mobilize more rapidly than Russia, he called for a holding action on the eastern front by a relatively small number of troops, thus allowing the use of a crushing force against France. The German left wing was to pivot on the fortified area near Metz. The powerful right wing was to follow the Meuse River valley through Belgium, pass Paris on the west, and fall upon the main French army from the rear. Moltke modified this plan to some extent. It was expected to take six weeks to complete the campaign. As the German armies smashed through Belgium, England entered the war. Despite the assistance of the British, the French fell back before the powerful drive of the German right wing. By Sept. 1, the Germans were 15 miles from Paris. The French government fled to Bordeaux. General Joffre, noting that the German right wing had lost contact with the rest of the army, launched the FIRST BATTLE OF THE MARNE (Sept. 6-10, 1914) (q.v.). The German drive was halted. The Germans retreated to the Aisne River, where they "dug in." After the Marne, there began a race between the Germans and the Allies to occupy the Channel Ports. The Germans captured most of these. But the British, in the First Battle of Ypres, kept control of a small part of southwest Flanders and the French ports of Calais, Dunkirk, and Boulogne. During the winter of 1914-15 the enemies consolidated their positions on the 600-mile front from Belgium to the Alps. Meanwhile, on the Eastern front, the Russians made surprising progress. Their rapid advance came to an abrupt end when they were decisively beaten by the Germans under Ludendorff and Hindenburg at Tannenberg (Aug. 26-31, 1914). This was followed by the rout of the Russians at the Masurian Lakes (Sept. 5-15, 1914) and at Augustovo (Feb. 1915). The Russians lost 1½ million men in these campaigns. Against Austria-Hungary the Russians were very successful, capturing most of Galicia and driving the defenders back to the Carpathian mountains. *1915.* The Central Powers drove the Russians out of Galicia. Bulgaria joined the Central Powers and helped in the conquest of Serbia. Italy entered the war on the side of the Allies (see Treaty of London). A Franco-British attack upon Constantinople by way of the Gallipoli Peninsula failed. On the western front the Allies made some progress in Flanders, but were repulsed in the Second Battle of Ypres, where on April 22, the Germans first successfully used poison gas. An Allied drive in the summer also failed. *1916*. This year was marked by two enormous campaigns: the German assault upon Verdun, from February to July: the Allied attack on the Somme, from June to November. Although the British used tanks in the Somme offensive, neither side possessed offensive weapons that were strong enough to effect a break-through. Both drives resulted in insignificant gains and tremendous casualty lists. The Austrians penetrated deep into the north of Italy, but had to withdraw when the Russians, under Brusilov, gained much ground in Galicia. The Russians were repulsed in a combined attack by the Central Powers, which also led to the conquest of Romania. *1917*. Early in 1917 the position of the Germans seemed to be fairly strong. They held Serbia, Montenegro, Romania, Poland, most of Belgium, and northern France. Russia was beaten down. Following the Red Revolution, in December, 1917, Russia also withdrew from the war. Three months later, (March 3rd, 1918) Russia signed the Treaty of Brest-Litovsk with the Germans and withdrew from the war in fact. However, in April 1917, the United States declared war on Germany. On the Western Front the Germans retired to the Hindenburg Line. In April, the British attacked at Arras and the French at Laon, without much success. From July to November the British fought the Third Battle of Ypres, eventually taking Passchendaele Ridge. On Oct. 24th, the Germans and Austrians launched a heavy attack on the Italian front, and hurled back the Italians with great losses. *1918*. On March 21, the Germans began a great offensive on the Western

Front. To cope with this menace, the Allies created a Supreme War Council and made General Foch commander-in-chief. The German drive was halted at Château-Thierry on July 18. Now the Allies began a counterattack in which the U.S. Army played a major role and which resulted in bringing the war to an end with an armistice, which was signed on November 11th. Colonial and Naval Operations. Kiaochow in China was captured by the Japanese in 1914. In the same year, British, Japanese, Australian, and New Zealand ships captured all the German islands in the Pacific. Togoland in Africa was captured by the British and French in 1914 and the Cameroons in 1916. German Southwest Africa was captured in 1915 by the Union of South Africa. Naval Operations consisted mainly of blockading action by the British and attempts of the Germans to break the blockade by use of the submarine.

World War II (1939-1945)   World War II was caused by the aggression of Japan, Italy, and Germany during the 1930's. This aggression was possible because of the failure of the League of Nations and because of the unwillingness of England, France, or the United States to resort to force to check it. When Germany and the USSR signed a non-aggression pact (Aug. 1939) (q.v.), the outbreak of war was inevitable. The war began Sept. 1, 1939, with the invasion of Poland by Germany. The Germans had demanded from Poland the city of Danzig and a strip of land through Polish territory which would unite East and West Prussia. When Poland refused this demand with the support of England and France, Germany began the invasion. The active fighting ended after 35 days, as the Russians moved in from the east, thus crushing Poland in a pincers movement (see Poland, Fifth Partition of). Now came a six-months period of inactivity known as the "PHONY-WAR"(q.v.) or "Sitzkrieg." During this period, Russia occupied the Baltic Republics of Estonia, Latvia, and Lithuania and engaged in a war with FINLAND (q.v.) to improve its boundaries. Active war resumed in April, 1940, when Germany invaded and crushed in rapid succession Denmark, Norway, Holland, Belgium, Luxemburg, and France. An English expeditionary force which had been serving in France was evacuated from Dunkirk in one of the most memorable operations of the war. France was partly occupied by the Germans. The remainder of the country was ruled from VICHY (q.v.). On August 8, 1940, began the "Battle of Britain." During the fall and winter of 1940 and the spring of 1941 the Luftwaffe (Nazi air force) tried to bring about the surrender of Britain through repeated aerial bombings. Coordinated with the air attack was a vicious submarine attack on ships which carried goods to the British Isles. The air attack became more intense in the spring as the days became longer and the skies clearer. On May 10, 1941, there was one final huge assault upon London during which the Houses of Parliament and the British Museum were damaged. After this great assault, the air attacks, which had resulted in enormous losses of German airplanes, tapered off as the Germans prepared for their attack upon Russia. Italy declared war against France and Great Britain on June 10, 1940. Italy launched two offensives: one against Greece and one against Egypt. Since neither attack succeeded, Germany was forced to come to Italy's assistance in both areas. Thus, Germany overran Yugoslavia and Greece in 1941 and launched General ROMMEL (q.v.) and his Afrika Korps on their spectacular career in North Africa. On June 22, 1941, the Germans invaded Russia. Although the blitzkrieg rolled into Russia in high gear and large areas of the country fell into Nazi hands, the campaign did not come to an end during this year as the Germans had hoped. On Dec.

7, 1941, the Japanese attacked the United States at Pearl Harbor. Thus the United States entered the war against the Axis. By mid-1942, the fortunes of the Axis reached their peak. The Germans had overrun most of southern Russia in Europe and invaded the oil fields of the Caucasus. In North Africa the Germans were in Egypt only 70 miles from the Suez Canal. Japan had captured all of Southeast Asia, the Philippine Islands, and the Dutch East Indies and were poised for the invasion of India and Australia. Then the tide of battle swung against the Axis. The British under General Montgomery turned back the Germans in Africa at El Alamein (Oct. 23, 1942). On Nov. 7, 1942, an Anglo-American expedition landed in North Africa. Thus the Germans were caught in a giant pincers and crushed in Tunis (May 8-12, 1943). In July, 1943, the Allies landed in Sicily and Italy. Mussolini's government fell and the new Italian government joined the Allies as a "co-belligerent." Meanwhile at Stalingrad (Aug. 22, 1942-Feb. 2, 1943) the attacking German army was encircled and forced to surrender. From that point on, the Nazis fought a defensive action on the Eastern Front. On June 6, 1944 (D-Day), the Allied troops under General Eisenhower established a bridgehead in Normandy. From there they fought on until the Germans surrendered, May 7, 1945. As Eisenhower's troops attacked and invaded Germany from the west, the Russians invaded from the east. Thus Germany was crushed between the forces of the United Nations. Starting with a landing on Guadalcanal in Aug. 1942, the Americans began the long "roadback" in the Pacific. War in the Pacific was largely a naval action with "island-hopping" from one strategic group of islands to another as the major feature of the plan of attack. In the final action of the war, the vital islands of Iwo Jima and Okinawa, both close to Japan, were captured. Atomic bombings on Hiroshima (Aug. 6, 1945) and Nagasaki brought the war to an end. Japan surrendered in Tokyo Bay, Aug. 14, 1945.

Y

Yalta Conference A meeting of President F. D. Roosevelt, Prime Minister Churchill, and Premier Stalin between February 4 and 11, 1945 at Yalta, Crimea, in the Soviet Union. The agreement provided for the following: common understanding to enforce UN-CONDITIONAL SURRENDER on Germany, a four power OCCUPATION OF GERMANY after the war (to include France which would be invited to participate), the destruction of militarism and Nazism, the DISARMA-MENT of German armed forces and the destruction of its general staff, the control of German Industry to prevent rearmament, the trial and punishment of all war criminals, a program of REPARATIONS, the elimination of Nazi and militarist influence from German society, and other measures to insure that Germany would thenceforth be prevented from embarking on war. The agreement also included a provision dealing with the terms under which the Soviet Union would enter the war against Japan, and arranged for the disposition of Japanese territories. Among these were Soviet consent to make war upon Japan not later than three months after Germany's surrender, and certain territorial adjustments which provided that the status quo be maintained in outer Mongolia, southern Sakhalin be restored to the Soviet Union, and that Dairen be internationalized with the recognition of the preeminent interests of the Soviet Union safeguarded by a lease of Port Arthur as a Soviet naval base. The Kurile Islands were to be returned to the Soviet Union, and the Chinese-Eastern and Southern-Manchurian railroads were to be jointly operated by a Soviet-Chinese Company. At Yalta the San Francisco Conference to inaugurate the United Nations was also planned.

Yoshida, Shigeru (1878) Japanese statesman. Prime Minister of Japan (1946, 1947, 1948-1954). Leader of the Liberal party.

Young Plan A plan of debt and REPARATIONS payment recommended in June, 1929 by a committee chaired by Owen D. Young. The Plan established a schedule of annual payments of reparations by Germany considered to be within her financial capacity. It established the Bank for International Settlements as the intermediary for acceptance and transfer of these payments. Under the Plan the total reparations bill was reduced to $8,000,000,000 and payment spread over a period of 58 years. It recognized the connection between reparations and allied war debts by providing that reparations payment could be reduced in the future in the same proportion that the United States reduced the war debts. The onset of the international DEPRESSION led to default by Germany. and in 1931 President HOOVER issued the Hoover Moratorium.

Ypres A subsidiary drive planned by the German general Ludendorff, following his first offensive in World War I was launched at Ypres in April, 1918. Poison gas was introduced here by German forces for the first time in modern warfare.

Z

Zimmermann Note (Jan. 19, 1917) German Foreign Secretary, Arthur Zimmermann, addressed a note to the German minister in Mexico, explaining that unrestricted submarine warfare was about to be resumed, but that efforts would be made to keep the United States neutral. Should these efforts fail, Germany was ready to propose an alliance with Mexico for a joint war against the United States. As a reward, Mexico was to regain some of the territory which it had lost to the United States. Japan was to be invited to join the alliance. The British intercepted this note and turned it over to the United States for publication. When it was made public, it strengthened the war fever in the United States, particularly in the Southwest.

Zinoviev Letter (Oct. 24, 1924) This letter was purported to have been written by Zinoviev, a Bolshevik leader, to British communists, urging the latter to prepare for revolution. It was published in England during a national election, and was directly responsible for the defeat of the first Labor Ministry. Later it appeared that the letter was a forgery.

Zionism A world movement whose purpose is the (a) establishment; (b) continuance of a Jewish National home. The first purpose has been fulfilled in the creation of the STATE OF ISRAEL.

BIBLIOGRAPHY

Brockway, Thomas P., *Basic Documents in United States Foreign Policy*. Princeton, 1957.

Carruth, Gordon, et al., *The Encyclopedia of American Facts and Dates*. New York, 1956.

Connell-Smith, Gordon, *Pattern of the Post-War World*. Baltimore, 1957.

Elliott, Florence and Michael Summerskill, *A Dictionary of Politics*. Baltimore, 1957.

Fairchild, Henry Pratt, *Dictionary of Sociology*. New York, 1944.

Jackson, J. Hampden, *The World in the Postwar Decade 1945-1955*. Boston, 1956.

Kirk, George E., *A Short History of the Middle East*. New York, 1957.

Langer, William L., *An Encyclopedia of World History*. Cambridge. 1956.

Lenczowski, George, *The Middle East in World Affairs*. Ithaca, 1956.

Littlefield, Henry W., *History of Europe since 1815*. New York, 1957.

Martin, Michael and Leonard Gelber, *Dictionary of American History*. New York, 1956.

Morris, Richard B., *Encyclopedia of American History*. New York, 1953.

McAuliffe, W. R., *Modern Asia Explained*. New York, 1952.

Reither, Joseph, *World History at a Glance*. New York, 1957.

Roeder, William S., *Dictionary of European History*. New York.

Roucek, Joseph S., *Slavonic Encyclopaedia*. New York, 1949.

Salvadori, Massimo, *NATO, A Twentieth-Century Community of Nations*. Princeton, 1957.

Smith, Edward Conrad and Arnold John Zurcher. *Dictionary of American Politics*. New York, 1957.

Steinberg, S. H., *Historical Tables 58 B.C.-A.D. 1945*. London, 1949.

Vinacke, Harold M., *A History of the Far East in Modern Times*. New York, 1950.

DATE DUE